POLICY AND PRACTICE IN EDUCATION

NUMBER SEVENTEEN

GENDER AND TEACHING:
WHERE HAVE ALL THE MEN GONE?

POLICY AND PRACTICE IN EDUCATION

POLICY AND PRACTICE IN EDUCATION

SERIES EDITORS
JIM O'BRIEN and CHRISTINE FORDE

GENDER AND TEACHING: WHERE HAVE ALL THE MEN GONE?

Sheila Riddell

Professor of Inclusion and Diversity
at the Moray House School of Education
University of Edinburgh

and

Lyn Tett

Professor of Community Education and Lifelong Learning
at the Moray House School of Education
University of Edinburgh

DUNEDIN ACADEMIC PRESS
EDINBURGH

Published by
Dunedin Academic Press Ltd
Hudson House
8 Albany Street
Edinburgh EH1 3QB
Scotland

ISBN 1 903765 57 9
ISBN 13: 978-1-903765-79-9
ISSN 1479-6910

British Library Cataloguing in Publication Data
A catalogue record for this book is available from the British Library

Typeset by Makar Publishing Production
Printed in Great Britain by Cromwell Press

Sheila and Lyn would like to dedicate this book
to the memory of their parents

CONTENTS

SERIES EDITORS' INTRODUCTION

The area of teacher policy is one of the emerging themes in this series. This volume explores the issue of the gender profile of the teaching profession as women, increasingly, make up the majority of teachers across all school sectors. As the authors argue 'teaching has always been a highly gendered profession' with gender differentiation evident in specific subjects, sectors and in school management. The authors illustrate, however, current trends with women moving into previously male dominated areas. In contrast, fewer men are coming into the teaching profession.

Sheila Riddell, Lyn Tett and their co-authors draw on a recently commissioned research project. The authors appraise simplistic notions that 'boys need men' critically but nevertheless highlight why the current trends in the gender balance of the teaching profession should be a matter of concern to both policy makers and practitioners. The authors examine the issues underlying this pattern by exploring the reasons why people choose teaching as a career and some of the reasons why others do not see teaching as a career option. The authors have gathered the views of teachers, of those directly involved in teacher education and in teacher policy development.

This book illuminates a number of significant issues concerning the gender balance in the teaching profession which face educational systems worldwide. On the basis of their analysis, the authors put forward a number of important points for policy makers. Against a backdrop of increasing demands and expectations on teachers, they raise the central question of how to make teaching an attractive career option.

Dr Jim O'Brien
Vice Dean and Director,
Centre for Educational Leadership,
Moray House School of Education,
The University of Edinburgh

Dr Christine Forde
Senior Lecturer in Educational Studies
The University of Glasgow

ACKNOWLEDGEMENTS

We would like to acknowledge the help and support we have received in conducting this research from the following individuals who were members of our Advisory Committee: Stewart Robertson, Scottish Executive Education Department; Anne Hunter, Scottish Executive Education Department; Veronica Rankine, Educational Institute of Scotland; and Dean Robson, General Teaching Council for Scotland.

Thanks are also due to Mal Cooke of the Scottish Executive for assistance with statistics. Catherine Burns at the Centre for Research in Education Inclusion and Diversity assisted in a range of ways throughout the research and in the production of this text and we are very grateful for her input. Finally, we would like to thank staff and students of the universities in which we conducted the undergraduate survey, all of our key informants and staff in the four schools who participated in the focus groups.

Chapter 1

SETTING THE SCENE

Sheila Riddell, Lyn Tett and Mandy Winterton

Introduction

Teaching is a highly gendered profession, both historically and currently. Historically, the ideology of the male breadwinner shaped not only social attitudes towards teachers, but also the pay and promotion structures that distributed unequal rewards to male and female staff. Between 1915 and 1945, local authority rules obliged women teachers to resign their posts on marriage, although married women whose husbands were unable to support them were allowed to be employed on a temporary basis (Adams, 1990). Differential pay scales for men and women in teaching were established in 1919, not to be removed until 1962 (Fewell, 1990). An argument used to justify these formal barriers to gender equality was the fear that women were taking over the profession and the absence of men as role models was likely to be detrimental to male pupils. Indeed, it has long been feared that the predominance of women in primary teaching is detrimental to boys' social, emotional and academic development and positive action in favour of men is necessary to halt the growing 'feminisation' of the teaching profession (Skelton, 2002; Acker, 1983). Debates about positive action in favour of men in the teaching profession have recently resurfaced in the light of concerns about the lack of adult male role models for underachieving boys, many of whom are socially disadvantaged (Tinklin *et al.*, 2001) and the growth of violence and indiscipline, also mainly involving disadvantaged boys (Mills, 2001) (see below for further discussion).

This book emerged from a Scottish Executive funded project on the gender balance of the teaching workforce in publicly funded schools in Scotland (Riddell *et al.*, 2005). It uses official statistics to describe and analyse the pattern of male and female participation (Chapter 2); analyses undergraduates' views of teaching as a future occupation (Chapter 3); discusses the views of careers officers and other key informants on how teaching should be promoted as a career (Chapter 4); and considers education professionals' accounts of the underlying reasons for the growing imbalance in teaching (Chapter 5). Finally, we return to a consideration of the key themes of the book and consider possible courses of action that might be taken to ensure greater diversity amongst the teaching workforce (Chapter 6). In this introductory chapter we set the scene in terms of the current policy context and indicate the central themes that weave through the following chapters.

The wider policy context

Within much of Europe and North America there is a desire to challenge gender stereotypes that are seen as outmoded and potentially restricting individual freedom and creativity. This can be interpreted positively as evidence of a growing concern within the developed world to ensure that women have access to social justice and human rights. Alternatively, and more cynically, it can be viewed as the desire to maximise the development and deployment of human capital, regardless of sex, in the context of advanced capitalism. Despite official commitment to equality, there is evidence of persistent inequality in women's and men's earnings which has proved quite resistant to change. Data published by the Women and Equality Unit (Dench *et al.*, 2002) show that the earnings gap between men and women in the UK has reduced considerably in the last 35 years. In 1970, the ratio of women's to men's earnings was 63 per cent, whereas by 2000, women earned 82 per cent of men's hourly full-time earnings. Since the early 1990s, the gap between women's and men's earnings has continued to narrow, but at a slower pace. In Scotland, the earnings ratio of women to men stands at around 81 per cent (Dench *et al.*, 2002). This is explained partly by the fact that part-time employees tend to be paid less, and women are far more likely to be working part-time then men. The earnings gap between women and men is lowest in areas where women predominate, for example, women in clerical and secretarial occupations earn 97.5 per cent of the wage of their male counterparts, and in professional occupations the earnings ratio is 91.1 per cent. The Equal Opportunities Commission has identified education as an area with a relatively small earnings gap compared with other professions.

Although the earnings gap is lower in female-dominated occupations, the overall salary level tends to be lower compared with comparable occupations where men are in the majority, and many occupations are still characterised by extremely marked gender divisions. The underlying reasons for the gendered nature of the labour market continue to be debated. Crompton (1997) analysed the alliance between the state and trades unions in promoting the idea of the family wage. Surviving until the latter part of the twentieth century, this ideology generally benefited men far more than women. Whilst there has been a rapid growth in female employment over the past two decades, horizontal and vertical segregation of occupation persists. At the same time, some changes are evident, with middle-class women entering professions which were previously dominated by men, such as law and medicine, and also making inroads into management in occupations such as banking, albeit in niche sectors such as call centres and personal finance (Crompton, 1997). The domestic division of labour also reveals a fairly fixed pattern, although it is clear that couples are more likely to share housework and childcare when the woman is in employment (Crompton, 1997).

Whilst the gendered division of labour has diminished, it has not entirely vanished and debates continue as to whether this is a result of material and economic factors (Hartmann, 1982; Walby, 1986) or women's and men's personal choices (Hakim, 1995, 1996). Hakim, drawing on data from large-scale surveys such as the Labour Force Survey and also from small-scale qualitative studies, has pointed out that women's orientation to the labour market is not uniform, with women having different levels of attachment to the world of work. According to Hakim (2004), about two- thirds of women have an adaptive/drifter approach to employment, with a parallel commitment to their family and domestic life. The other third are split between a maternalist/family centred orientation, which prioritises the family role, and the work-centred orientation, which places employment at the centre. Hakim suggests that there is a growing polarisation between women at opposite ends of this spectrum, who often make very different political demands and, at least in the USA, have formed competing women's movements. Like women, men's commitment to the labour market varies, with some men being far more ambitious and work-centred than others. However, whereas women cluster in the adaptive/drifter middle of the continuum, men are far more likely to be work-orientated and very few men would be found at the family-orientated end of the spectrum, evidenced, for example, by Swedish men's reluctance to make use of quite generous paternity leave (Gordon, 2006). This, Hakim points out, is partly because men may have less freedom than women to choose their particular position in the labour market, there being a heavy social expectation that men will work from the point at which they leave full-time education to their retirement.

Feminist sociologists of employment, whilst often accepting Hakim's account of the spectrum of orientations to employment, disagree strongly with the underlying mechanisms structuring the gendered division of labour. In particular, they take issue with the individuation arguments propounded by Beck (1992; 1998), which suggest that the individual is the author of his or her destiny, in the labour market as elsewhere. For example, Siltanen (1986) argued that many women expect their salary to represent a constituent element of a household income, rather than being sufficient to support an entire household, but suggests that this is a result of underpinning social, cultural and economic factors, rather than unalloyed free choice. Critics of Hakim suggest that her position plays into the hands of conservatives who oppose equal opportunities measures and positive action strategies in work-places.

These debates are not only academic, but may also provide important explanations for the differences which are currently emerging in men's and women's attitudes to teaching as a career. Such analysis also highlights the dynamic nature of the relationship of men and women to the labour market, and the extent to which rapid change has taken place over the last few decades. It is clear that change takes place partly as a result of shifting economic and social relationships, but also as a result of changing atti-tudes and personal choices, which may not always be synchronised with economic cycles. In order to shift the current gender balance in teaching, it is therefore necessary to address not only the formal and informal barriers to equality which remain, but also to understand the reasons behind the choices made by women and men, which may not always be rational. One of the aims of the study was thus to develop a better understanding of the work orientations of potential recruits to teaching (undergraduate students) and practising teachers. Did women who were already in teaching posts, or who were contemplating teaching as a career, have different views of employment compared with their male counterparts? And if so, how might this be understood?

Government equality policies
As noted above, equality of opportunity and human rights are high on the social, political and intellectual agenda, although there is often a lack of clarity about what is meant by equality. Recent policy developments, including the publication of the White Paper *Fairness for All* (DTI, 2005) and the passage of the Equality Act 2006, have emphasised the principle of mainstreaming equality. The need to implement European Employment Directives has led to new Regulations in the area of religion and belief, sexual orientation and age discrimination. Public and private sector organisations have new duties to ensure that they do not discriminate against their staff (and students in the case of educational institutions) on six grounds (gender, race, disability, age, sexual orientation and religion/belief). There is also a growing emphasis not just on the need to avoid discrimination, but also to positively promote equality. The Race Relations (Amendment) Act 2000 placed a duty on public sector bodies to positively promote equality in relation to race, and a similar duty applies to disability from 2006 and gender from 2007. The Commission for Equality and Human Rights (CEHR) will be established in 2007, with the aim of ensuring that public and private sector organisations place equal opportunities at the centre of all their activities.

In Scotland, equality policy has a wider ambit than these six strands. The Scotland Act (1998) defines equal opportunities in terms of 'the prevention, elimination or regulation of discrimination between persons on grounds of sex or marital status, on racial grounds, or on grounds of disability, age, sexual orientation, language or social origin, or of other personal attributes, including beliefs or opinions, such as religious beliefs or political opinions'. In Scotland, therefore, equalities law is a complex mix of European, UK and Scottish legislation and policy.

These radical changes in approaches to equalities in Scotland have particular consequences for the public sector, including education. The Scottish Executive Education Department and local authorities have new duties to monitor the gender balance of the teaching profession closely and set targets for the gradual eradication of gender differences. Clearly, this represents a stiff challenge, since currently gender differences are tending to solidify, rather than diminish. This is in contrast to other sectors such as higher education, where there are growing numbers of women and the gender imbalance is decreasing, albeit with relatively slow progress at more senior levels. If the duty to reduce gender imbalance is to be taken seriously, this raises questions about what actions are likely to be effective. An aim of this book is not simply to describe, but also to increase understanding of the reasons underpinning men's and women's decisions to enter teaching or, alternatively, to reject it as a career option, with a view to identifying what types of action might yield positive outcomes for both women and men.

The international decline of men in teaching
Given the flurry of activity around equality and human rights, it is paradoxical that, far from melting away, gender divisions within school education appear to be hardening, with women moving into areas previously colonised by men such as secondary education and management. This can, of course, be read as evidence of women's increasing social empowerment, or of their relative lack of power, as they undertake jobs which men no longer see as valuable.

The teacher census carried out by the Scottish Executive Education Department in 2003 showed that there had been a fall in the percentage of teachers who were male from 30 per cent in 1998 to 26 per cent in 2003. With regard to initial teacher education (ITE), men made up only 10 per cent of entrants to primary education in 2002–03, and 39 per cent of entrants to secondary education (see Chapter 2 for further discussion). This gender imbalance is evident in many European countries and other parts of the developed world (UNESCO, 2003; Drudy *et al.*, 2005). Tables 1.1 and 1.2 show this wider picture. Table 1.2 allows contrasts to be drawn between countries which are relatively rich or poor. Whereas poor countries have a high proportion of men in primary teaching (e.g. in Bangladesh, 62 per cent of primary teachers are men), in rich countries such as the USA a far smaller proportion of primary teachers are men (12 per cent). In the Russian Federation, gender divisions appear particularly marked, so that only 2 per

Gender and Teaching

Table 1.1: Percentage full-time women teachers by sector, 2002/03 EU

	Primary	**Lower Secondary**	**Upper Secondary**
YEAR / COUNTRY	2002/03	2002/03	2002/03
Austria	90	67	50
Belgium	78	58	...
Finland	75	72	...
France	81	64	52
Germany	83	60	43
Italy	95	75	58
Luxembourg	69	...	...
Spain	70	...	...
Sweden	80	63	51
United Kingdom	81	59	60

Source: UNESCO, *World Education Report 2003*

Table 1.2: Percentage full-time women teachers by sector, 2002/03 International

	Primary	**Lower Secondary**	**Upper Secondary**
YEAR / COUNTRY	2002/2003	2002/2003	2002/2003
Bangladesh	38	14	15
Brazil	90	86	69
China	53	45	41
India	44	37	32
Japan	65	40	25
Kenya	41	...	...
Mexico	63	48	41
New Zealand	87	66	...
Nicaragua	82	56	56
Nigeria	48	38	38
Pakistan	36	...	...
Russian Federation	98	...	...
United States	88	65	55

Source: UNESCO, *World Education Report 2003*

cent of primary teachers are male. In the secondary sector, the same general pattern applies, although the proportion of men is generally higher. As a general rule, it would appear that across the world, where jobs are scarce, men are attracted to teaching, particularly in the secondary sector, but where other jobs become available, the proportion of men in teaching declines. In support of this argument, Drudy *et al.* (2005) note that in Ireland, whilst the economy was relatively depressed in the 1980s, men continued to represent a significant majority of all secondary school teachers. In the economic boom days of the 1990s, however, men appeared to be less inclined to go into teaching at either primary or secondary level. The interesting question here is perhaps why women continue to be attracted to teaching when, like men, they might pursue other job options.

Whilst women continue to dominate in primary teaching in developed countries and their numbers are increasing in secondary education, men continue to hold most management positions, as Table 1.3 demonstrates.

Table 1.3: Percentage of women among management staff in primary and secondary education, 1999/2000

	Primary	**Lower Secondary**	**Upper Secondary**	**All Secondary**
Belgium (Flemish community)	31.5			22.9
France	80	54	58.4	
Ireland	49			32.7
Netherlands	14			13.4
Austria	46.4	15.3	11.3	
Finland	34.3	31.8	30.4	
Sweden	72.1	31.8	30.4	
UK	59.7			30
Iceland	40.1			25.8
Norway	44.4			32.6
Cyprus	52.4			40
Malta	54.7	36.5	54	
Slovenia	57.5	56.1	49	
Estonia	69.8			69.8

Source: European Union, *Key Data on Education in Europe, 2002*

In most European countries, it appears that there is an association between the age group of children and the proportion of female heads, with schools for young children having a lower proportion of male head teachers. France has a very high proportion of female head teachers (80 per cent), whilst the Netherlands has only 14 per cent. The Netherlands also has a low proportion of female head teachers in secondary schools (13.4 per cent). Estonia has a high proportion of female head teachers across the board (69.8 per cent). Clearly, very specific economic, social and cultural factors underpin these national differences. However, across Europe and richer developed countries there has been a slow but steady increase in the proportion of women in school management over the past decade.

At this point, we will review the key themes of the book which are interwoven in the following chapters and revisited in the conclusion.

The central themes of the book

Gender, identity and employment

Feminist writing in the 1970s drew an important distinction between 'sex' and 'gender' (Oakley, 1981). Whereas sex referred to biological difference, gender denoted a socially and culturally constructed category, infinitely diverse and varying across place and time. This type of thinking led to entirely new ways of understanding relations between men and women, although much feminist writing of the 1970s stuck to analyses of the part played by institutions such as schools in sex role socialisation (e.g. Adams and Laurikietis, 1980), geared to fitting men and women into their future locations in the family and the labour market. During the 1980s and 1990s, a body of work developed which tried to interrogate the ways in which women and men negotiated gender identities within specific social structures. Strongly influenced by Paul Willis' neo-marxist account of working class boys' relationship to schooling (Willis, 1976), researchers questioned the ways in which social class and gender were reproduced through individuals' negotiation of identity (Gaskell, 1992; Connell, 1989; Riddell, 1992). The notion of identity negotiation tended to replace the earlier concept of sex role socialisation, which became derided for its functionalist and deterministic connotations.

Debates continue about the degrees of freedom available to individuals in negotiating their pathways through life. Theorists of late modernity, such as Ulrich Beck, have made the case for the intrepid individual forging his or her own identity through the negotiation of global and personal risks:

> Increasingly everyone has to choose between different options, including as to which group or subculture one wants to be identified with. In fact one has to choose and change one's social identity as well and take the risks in doing so. (Beck, 1992, p. 88)

In his later writing, Beck acknowledges the persistence of class patterns, resulting in the poor attracting 'an unfortunate abundance of risks' (Beck, 1992, p. 35). Skeggs, on the other hand, argues for the continued salience of social class in influencing individuals' life chances and experiences:

> The individualism which is assumed in a great deal of theorising on subjectivity is the product of, and in the interests of, privileged groups in very specific national and historical circumstances . . . Concepts of individualism legitimate powerful groups and render other groups unworthy of the designation 'individual'. (Skeggs, 1997, p. 163)

These debates have practical significance in terms of how we understand individuals' educational and employment decisions. Are women social and cultural dupes in continuing to opt into teaching as a career, a job which appears to have been rejected by a significant body of men as too hard and insufficiently well remunerated? On the other hand, are there clear reasons for women continuing to see teaching as a potential field of employment?

Earlier writing in the field of gender and careers provides interesting insights into the ways in which women's dominance of the teaching profession has tended to be problematised. Sandra Acker (1983) provided a compelling account of the way in which sociological analyses of the teaching profession up to the early 1970s tended to characterise women as 'damaging, deficient, distracted and sometimes even dim' (Acker, 1983, p. 124). Etzioni (1969) categorised teaching as one of the 'semi-professions', alongside social work, nursing and librarianship. According to Acker, the woman-blaming character of Etzioni's edited collection is exemplified in the chapter by Richard and Ida Simpson. According to the Simpsons:

> A woman's primary attachment is to the family role; women are therefore less intrinsically committed to work than men and less likely to maintain a high level of specialised knowledge. Because their work motives are more utilitarian and less intrinsically task-orientated than those of men, they may require more control. Women's stronger competing attachment to their family roles and to their clients make them less likely than men to develop colleague reference group orientations. For these reasons, and because they often share the general cultural norm that women defer to men, they are more willing than men to accept the bureaucratic controls imposed upon them in semi-professional organisations, and less likely to seek a genuinely professional status. (Simpson and Simpson, 1969, cited in Acker, 1983, p. 125)

Sociological research conducted after the mid-1970s, Acker argues, influenced by symbolic interactionism and second wave feminist writing, tends to be more nuanced and less accusatory, focusing on the ways in which men and women make sense of the idea of a career in teaching (e.g. Lortie, 1975). One finding from Lortie's study which, Acker suggests, may still have considerable salience is that the small number of men in primary teaching included in the sample had low commitment to and interest in their work, but all hoped to be principals over the next five years.

Overall, Acker concludes that most sociological writing on the influence of gender on teachers' careers has the following shortcomings:

1. a deficit model of women that leads to a blame-the-victim approach as well as conceptual confusion;

2. what appears to be a low regard for the intellectual capacities of teachers, perhaps especially women teachers;
3. a persistent tendency to see women exclusively in family role terms;
4. a poor sense of history coupled with an inability to anticipate social change;
5. an over-simplified view of causality;
6. a pervasive ideology of individual choice, deeply embedded in American writing about women's work and often uncritically applied in British literature.

In the light of Acker's analysis, it is interesting to consider the extent to which the current concern around the 'feminisation' of teaching is driven by an underlying suspicion of women's professionalism and a view that they are responsible for the low status of teaching as a profession.

The ongoing debate in the literature on gender and employment, discussed above, is relevant to the issue of career choice identified by Acker. Whereas writers like Siltanen (1986) have tended to emphasise structural barriers, others such as Hakim (1996; 2002; 2004) have sought to debunk 'feminist myths' and have played up the salience of women's personal choices. According to Hakim, denying that women exercise some degree of agency in their educational and employment decisions is dangerous because it implicitly denigrates women's priorities and re-establishes the idea of the male as norm. On the basis of the evidence presented in forthcoming chapters, we consider the explanations given by women and men for their decisions to become a teacher, or their rejection of teaching as a possible career route.

The decline of men in teaching and the 'problem of boys'
There is a major concern throughout developed countries with the poorer academic performance of boys in schools compared with that of girls. In Scotland, as elsewhere, boys are generally performing worse than girls, gaining an average of 35 points at Standard Grade in 1998 compared with girls, who attain 39 points on average (Tinklin *et al.*, 2001). It is, however, important to note that the average attainment gap between girls and boys is considerably smaller than the attainment gap between pupils of different social classes, suggesting that gender differences should not be the sole cause of anxiety. Boys are also more likely than girls to be identified as having special or additional educational needs, excluded from school and placed in special schools and units. In 2004, 70 per cent of pupils with SEN, 68 per cent of pupils attending special schools and 79 per cent of those excluded from schools were male (Scottish Executive 2005a, 2005b). These differences may well relate to a greater identification of boys as having particular impairments than girls: for example, in such categories as social,

emotional and behavioural difficulties (SEBD), autistic spectrum disorder, and moderate learning difficulties (Scottish Executive, 2005a). Gender differentials are not always negative for boys. For example, more boys are likely to be categorised as having specific learning difficulties (71 per cent of this category) (Scottish Executive, 2005a) and this may give them assistance of scribes or readers and (possibly) lower university entrance level qualifications (Riddell *et al.*,1994). These patterns hold true across many developed and developing countries (OECD, 2005), prompting questions about possible causes. Noting the global pattern that more boys then girls are being identified as having special educational needs and are receiving additional resources to access the curriculum, the OECD suggested that one possible causal factor is that 'schooling is becoming increasingly feminised' (OECD, 2005, p. 140).

The 'problem' of the feminisation of teaching has been discussed from a range of perspectives, with many writers expressing considerable suspicion of the idea that women teachers are automatically bad for boys, and conversely male teachers are intrinsically preferable. Weiner *et al.* (2001), Francis (1999) and Gray and Leith (2004) all identify a variety of research showing how the school system currently and historically favours boys, particularly in terms of the distribution of teacher time in the classroom. Mac an Ghaill (1994), Connell (1996) and Mills (2001) all point out the importance of dominant forms of masculinity emanating from boys' peer groups in school, which may be far more influential than teachers themselves. Interestingly, Mills (2001) and Mills *et al.* (2004) suggest that encouraging men to engage in anti-sexist work with boys in schools might have some positive outcomes, but could actually be counter-productive depending on the version of masculinity which is being promoted. They are particularly wary of some of the thinking in the men's movement exemplified by American writers such as Robert Bly (1991), who draw on 'mytho-poetic' traditions to argue that in the modern world men are victimised because of restrictions on their right to access and express their 'deep masculinities'.

There are therefore two specific and possibly competing strands in the literature which make connections between boys' apparent difficulties in the education system and the declining proportions of male teachers. On the one hand, there is an assumption that the reduction in the number of men in teaching is linked causally to the boys' attainment and behavioural difficulties. The suggestion springing from such arguments is that the way to improve the situation for boys is to take active steps to employ more male teachers and encourage them to work with boys, particularly those from lone parent families and disadvantaged backgrounds. On the other hand, another body of work suggests that, whilst anti-sexist work in schools may be valuable to both boys and girls, the underlying political understandings and actions of those undertaking such work is more important than their sex. Indeed, men committed to certain types of masculinist thinking might actually make matters worse rather than better by promoting unhelpful forms of masculinity that denigrate women. In this study we asked our respondents how they felt that these competing discourses might be resolved and if they considered that the decline of men in teaching was an issue that should be tackled by taking positive action to recruit more men.

Gender, education and new managerialism
Since the mid-1980s, public services in Scotland and the rest of the UK have been transformed by the linked influences of marketisation and managerialism. Newman describes the principles of New Public Management thus:

> New Public Management was a term used to describe a series of reforms which reshaped the relations between public and private sectors, professionals and managers, and central and local government. Citizens and clients were recast as consumers and public service organisations were recast in the image of the business world. (Newman, 2000)

Performance management was increasingly emphasised, with targets being used to assess individual and service performance. Regulatory systems meant that management could be devolved to local level whilst still being controlled from the centre. In addition, accountability regimes were intended not only to ensure service effectiveness and efficiency, but also to allow consumers of public services to choose between competing providers, thus fuelling markets. Public service professionals, rather than being distinct from managers, were increasingly co-opted into managerial roles (Exworthy and Halford, 1999).

As managerialism in the public sector progressed, fears were expressed by feminist writers that women might find it more, rather than less, difficult to gain promotion (Mahony, 2000; Rees *et al.*, 2000; Skelton, 2003). Mahony (2000) suggested that the criteria used to appoint future managers were likely to reflect characteristics associated with masculinity such as authority, discipline and control. Head teachers would increasingly be held responsible for pupil achievement and staff compliance with curricular requirements. Hierarchical management structures, as opposed to democratic and consensual practices which might once have existed in primary schools, were likely to fit more easily with a male *modus operandi*. Furthermore, there was a perceived danger that, in order for women to progress in such circumstances, their psychological well-being might be compromised:

> If successful management is defined in masculinist terms then women will be pressured to conform to its dictates in ways which may create

tensions between their values and their power to act in collaborative ways. (Mahony, 2000, p. 238)

Dualism of male competitiveness versus female collegiality pervades much of this literature and there are dangers of slipping into essentialist thinking, assuming that men and women are two homogenous groups, an approach criticised by a number of commentators (Hay and Bradford, 2004; Sachs and Blackmore, 1998). Managerial sex typing may over-simplify the diverse nature of managerial styles within and between the sexes. Coleman (2002) found younger female heads believed that 'male' managerial qualities were equally likely to be exhibited by women and men, and many male head teachers identified their own managerial style as lying within a feminine managerialist paradigm. However, research on management styles using psychometric data (Adler, 1994, cited in Coleman, 2002) suggests that men may be less collaborative than they believe themselves to be. Coleman (2002) and Sachs and Blackmore (1998) present a more complex picture of female teachers, with reminders that some women, like some men, may behave in a highly adversarial manner (Sachs and Blackmore, 1998).

Again, there is something of a paradox here, since far from deterring women from entering management positions in education, the advent of managerialism appears to have coincided with an increase in women managers in schools, although of course that does not imply a causal relationship. A focus of the research was therefore to examine the reaction of practising male and female teachers to the managerialist regimes which increasingly surround them in schools.

A strong focus on inclusion has been a further feature of education policy since the election of a New Labour government at Westminster and the establishment of the Scottish Parliament in 1999 (Tisdall and Riddell, 2006) The Scottish Executive has funnelled considerable monies towards local authorities and their schools to promote this goal. For example, funds have been put aside for Alternatives to Exclusion, to raise standards in Scotland's schools (the Excellence Fund), and Special Educational Needs Innovation Grants. A major educational initiative in 1998 was to pilot New (now Integrated) Community Schools, which sought to provide integrated services to children, and was directly linked to the social justice agenda. Finally, the Discipline Task Group in its report *Better Behaviour–Better Learning* (Scottish Executive, 2001) recommended that funds be allocated to local authorities to enable the employment of additional staff, such as classroom assistants and home-school link workers, to support positive behaviour. Initiatives such as the restorative practices pilot (McCluskey *et al.*, 2006) have sought to transform school culture, shifting the emphasis from punishment to conflict resolution. Evidence from the restorative practices evaluation indicates that, whilst many teachers favour these new developments, they are less popular in the secondary sector and particularly with men (McCluskey *et al.*, 2006).

Attracting more men into teaching

Our final theme arises from the issues raised by the preceding theme as attracting more men into teaching may not have the desired effects of improving the profession. For example, Reynolds' (2001) research shows the limitation of a simplistic assumption of male teachers' capacity to reach out to under-achieving boys. Her ethnographic research showed the importance of boys adapting their behaviours and activities to gain acceptance by the hegemonic group of boys, and also the difficulties for those boys who were unable to do this. The research concluded that the male role model initiative seemed only to be directed at the under-achieving boys displaying aggressive forms of masculinity, completely overlooking the non-rebellious under-achievers. So whilst men should be encouraged to work with boys in identifying and challenging negative aspects of macho culture, positive action to encourage men into teaching will not automatically ensure that boys' problems are resolved.

On the other hand, research (Drudy *et al.*, 2005) shows that many parents see male teachers as beneficial, providing a more positive role model to counteract many media portrayals of men as violent and unemotional. However, there is some concern that recruitment drives aimed overtly at men might reinforce established stereotypes of masculinity, and therefore could be detrimental to achieving gender equality in education. They may also reinforce an approach to boy's problem behaviour that views female teachers as not as capable of teaching boys whereas the issue to be addressed is the way in which gendered relations of power are enacted between boys and female teachers (see Mills *et al.*, 2004). Similarly, advertising specifically to attract men, for example, by drawing attention to the fact that men still occupy the highest paid jobs in teaching, might reinforce negative gender stereotypes from the outset, attract competitive careerist men, and possibly lead to the denigration of female teachers (Carrington and Skelton, 2003).

In this study, one of our aims was to identify suggestions from a range of informants about whether the declining proportion of men should be seen as a problem, and if so, how it should be tackled without explicitly or implicitly undermining women.

Research methods

Research methods used included a literature and policy review; an analysis of Scottish statistics from a range of sources including the Scottish Executive, the General Teaching Council for Scotland (GTCS) and the Scottish Higher Education Funding Council; key informant interviews; a survey of undergraduates on social and biological science programmes in three

Scottish universities; interviews with university careers service staff; and focus groups with practising teachers in primary and secondary schools. The following table summarises data gathered during the course of the research.

Table 1.4: Summary of data sources

Type of data	Source/Group	Number
Official statistics	Secondary analysis of Scottish Executive teacher census	
Key informant interviews	Head teachers and representatives from the Scottish Executive, Her Majesty's Inspectorate of Education (HMIE), local authorities, the GTCS, teacher unions, ITE course directors	18
Focus groups	Male and female teachers at different career stages and in different subject areas working in different parts of Scotland	4 schools (2 primary, 2 secondary). 2 focus groups in each secondary and one in each primary school (i.e. 6 focus groups in all)
Interviews with university careers staff		3 (1 in each university)
Undergraduate survey	Third year undergraduates in arts/social science and science/maths	Survey administered in 3 universities. 2 student groups per university. 323 questionnaires returned

Full details of research methods are given in the appropriate chapter.

Summary and conclusion

The study reported in this book set out to examine the pattern of men's and women's participation in the teaching force in Scotland, the reasons underlying the growing gender imbalance, the implications for the system as a whole and the steps which might be taken to encourage greater gender equality in the future. In this introductory chapter, we have sketched the broad policy context and outlined the key themes of the book. An important element of the backdrop is that, at a time when the Scottish and UK governments are actively promoting equality and human rights, there is evidence of growing gender inequality in education, which is clearly a key area of public policy. This is not only a Scottish issue, but is reflected throughout the developed world. The situation of developing countries provides some interesting points of comparison, in that where jobs are scare, teaching appears to attract men, who move into alternative occupations as the economy grows and alternative occupations emerge. Given the new public sector duty to actively promote gender equality, serious questions emerge about what actions can be taken by national and local government, as well as individual schools to redress the gender imbalance without discriminating against women.

In exploring the underlying reasons for the continued attraction of teaching to women as opposed to its rejection by men, three overlapping themes are addressed throughout the book. These concern the part played by occupational choice in the negotiation of identity, the impact of new managerialism on experiences of teaching, the suggested link between the decline of men in teaching and the problem of boys and what actions, if any, should be taken to address the gender imbalance. In the next chapter we provide a view of the current picture of those in teacher training and in the teaching workforce in Scotland and consider the changes over recent times.

Chapter 2

GENDER BALANCE IN THE TEACHING WORKFORCE: OFFICIAL STATISTICS

Joanna Ferrie and Sheila Riddell

Introduction

In this chapter we discuss the balance of women and men in the teaching workforce and in teacher training in Scotland, considering changes over time. The aim is to identify the extent of the decline in the proportion of men in particular sectors and subject areas and the implications of these changes for the curriculum and the education system as a whole. We also analyse the number of women entering teaching by sector and subject area, and consider why women have not been deterred from teaching as appears to be the case for men, a discussion which is continued in Chapters 4 and 5. The extent of the current imbalance of men and women in management positions in Scottish education is also discussed, and prospects for change in traditional hierarchies are considered. Most data were drawn from the Scottish Executive teacher census, but some were supplied by the General Teaching Council for Scotland.

Gender balance in the professions in Scotland

It is important to consider the position of men and women in teaching in the context of a wider analysis of gender and the professions in Scotland. Kay (2001) analysed the representation of women in a number of professional spheres including the following: natural science, engineering, health, teaching, law, service occupations (housing, social work, librarianship), administration and management, environmental management. The analysis was based on published statistical data. Even though the Labour Force Survey shows an increase in women's participation in employment in Scotland since 1990, with some of this increase in the professions, most professional groups do not collect and publish information to allow comparisons to be made over time. Particularly in the light of new equality legislation, greater transparency will be needed in the future. Data that are available show that there are a higher proportion of women in the lower grades than in the higher grades in all professions. In some areas, for example natural science and engineering, there are only a small number of women amongst the professional body, with little change over the past decade. In professions where women are better represented, the gender imbalance in the higher echelons is marked. So, for example, at the time of Kay's research, women made up about a quarter of those conducting actuarial work, but the proportion of women fellows remained at about one in ten. In law, whilst women account for about half the number of solicitor employees, fewer than one in five becomes a partner. Some organisations have been much more active than others in taking steps to encourage women to enter non-traditional areas and subsequently to seek promotion. So, for example, in engineering the government has supported initiatives such as *Women into Science and Engineering* and *Winning Women*. Family-friendly policies have been pursued most vigorously in areas where women are already a majority. Nursing, for example, is a predominantly female profession, but there are proportionately more men in senior posts. The Royal College of Nursing has actively promoted family-friendly policies, and continues to address issues such as women's health at work and career progression. Generally, 'family friendly practices' appear to be geared to helping women in professions, rather than assisting men to achieve a better work–life balance.

The proportion of men and women in Scottish schools

Let us now look more closely at the position of women in teaching. In 2003, there were 49,230 teachers employed to work in 2,826 publicly funded schools teaching 406,015 pupils. Of these 55 per cent taught in primary schools, 44 per cent taught in secondary schools and 1 per cent taught in special schools. Figure 2.1 shows that the majority of both male and female

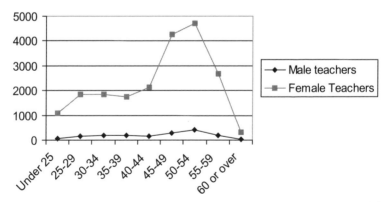

Figure 2.1: Scottish primary school teachers in 2003 by age and gender (Scottish Executive, 2004)

teachers are over the age of 44. This suggests that the problem of teacher supply is not only related to attracting more men into teaching, but also to sustaining the number of women entering the profession.

The number of primary teachers in the 45+ age groups, the majority of whom are women, is clearly an issue which the Scottish Executive has been considering in planning teacher supply. If all these teachers retire at 60 or over, then 58 per cent of all primary teachers will have retired in the next 15 years (Scottish Executive, 2004). Statistics published in 2005 (Scottish Executive, 2005a) but relating to the academic session 2002–2003, revealed that in that year teachers were twice as likely to take early retirement (n=707) than continue working until the official retirement age (n =374). An additional 174 retired early on health grounds.

In every year from 1996 to 2003, there were almost five times as many female primary school teachers as male primary school teachers. There were also consistently more female secondary school teachers than male teachers, although the gap in the secondary sector was much smaller. However, Figure 2.2 shows that the gap in the number of male and female teachers is widening, as the absolute number of female teachers increases and the number of male teachers declines.

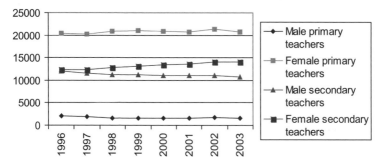

Figure 2.2: Teachers by gender and type of school 1996–2003 (Scottish Executive, 2004) Note: No official figures were available by gender before 1996.

An individual-level teacher census was conducted in 1992, 1994 and 1998, then annually from 2003. In all years prior to 2003, there were also school-level summary censuses which gave teacher numbers, which from 1996 onwards can be reliably split into male/female. Figure 2.3 summarises the number and percentages of teachers in different sectors by gender.

Statistical analysis showed that there were significantly fewer men teaching in primary schools in 2003 compared with 1994. Significant differences were also detected between all three years examined for men teaching in secondary schools. There were significantly fewer men teaching in 1998

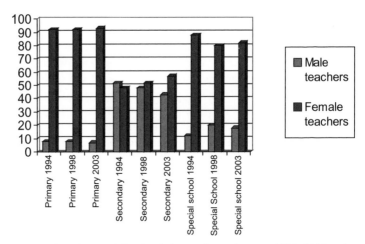

Figure 2.3: Teachers in Scottish schools by gender and sector, 1994, 1998 and 2003 (percentages) (Scottish Executive, 2004)

compared with 1994, and fewer teaching in 2003 compared with 1998. A similar pattern was detected, as expected, for women teaching in secondary schools in Scotland. There were significantly more women teaching in secondary schools in 1998 compared with 1994, and more women teaching in secondary schools in 2003 compared with 1998. It would appear that primary teaching has always been, and continues to be, a female-dominated sphere. Secondary school teaching, on the other hand, where there used to be a majority of men, is now becoming an increasingly female-dominated area, although the imbalance is not nearly as great as in the primary sector. Interesting questions arise here with regard to push and pull factors. Are men failing to enter teaching because more attractive options are available, and if so, why are these alternatives not equally attractive to women? Alternatively, are men being deterred by features of teaching, and if so, why are these push factors not being reacted to in the same way by women?

The ethnicity of teachers in Scottish schools

Particularly in the light of moves to consider the inter-sections of equality strands as a matter of routine, rather than seeing them in isolation from each other, it is important to consider teachers' ethnicity as well as their gender. It is evident that the teaching profession in Scotland at the moment is overwhelmingly white (see Table 2.1), indeed all principal, depute and head primary teachers who declared their ethnicity on the census described themselves as white-UK or white-other. According to the 2001 Census, about 2 per cent of the total population of Scotland was from minority ethnic groups, a higher proportion than in the 1991 Census (Scottish Executive, 2004). Since the minority ethnic population is likely to increase further over time, it will obviously be important for the Scottish Executive and local authorities to check that this growth is reflected in the composition of the teaching profession.

Table 2.1: Primary school teachers by ethnicity and grade, 2003 (Scottish Executive, 2004)

	Head Teacher	Depute Head	Principal Teacher	Teacher	Percentage overall
White – UK	2,052	1,372	604	17,027	94.7
White – other	26	18	10	328	1.7
Mixed				13	0.03
Asian – Indian				14	0.05
Asian – Pakistani				16	0.07
Asian – Bangladeshi					…
Asian – Chinese					…
Asian – other					…
Black – Caribbean					…
Black – African					…
Black – other				16	0.07
Other				18	0.08
Not disclosed	42	45	14	663	3.3

Gender and promotion

As noted in Chapter 1, whilst the trend in Scotland and internationally is for a decline in the proportion of men and a growth in the proportion of women in teaching, management posts in education continue to be male-dominated. As illustrated in Figure 2.4, men's chances of becoming head teachers in Scotland are still considerably better than those of women.

Men make up only 7 per cent of the primary school workforce, but 20 per cent of head teachers, and in secondary, they represent 43 per cent of the workforce, but 82 per cent of head teachers. Men teaching in primary and secondary schools are five times more likely to be head teachers than their female counterparts and men working in special schools are almost twice as likely to be head teachers as women. Clearly, even though there is a downward trend in the number of men going into teaching, the odds of gaining promotion are still stacked in their favour. There are some signs that this may change in the near future, since about two thirds of candidates for the Standard for Headship are now women (see Table 2.2 below):

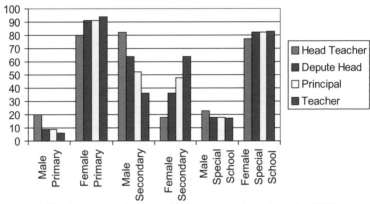

Figure 2.4: Teachers by grade, type of school, seniority and gender 2003 (percentages) (Scottish Executive, 2004)

Table 2.2: Number of women and men undertaking the Scottish Qualification for Headship 2004

Year	Women	Men	Total
2001	118	47	165
2002	95	54	149
2003	97	55	152
2004	117	42	159
Total	427	198	**625**

Close monitoring will again be important, since undertaking this qualification does not automatically translate into obtaining a promoted post. It is also worth noting that men occupy an even higher proportion of positions higher up in education management and administration. Within local authority education directorates (often now combined with children's and cultural services), 90 per cent of Directors are men (29 out of 32 in May 2006).

Gender and subject taught

Figure 2.5 shows subject taught by gender for secondary school teachers in the fifteen subjects with the largest number of teachers. Clearly, most curriculum areas are still heavily dominated by either men or women, and the proportion of girls and boys in particular subjects is almost a mirror image of the gender of staff working in that area (see Figures 2.6 and 2.7 below).

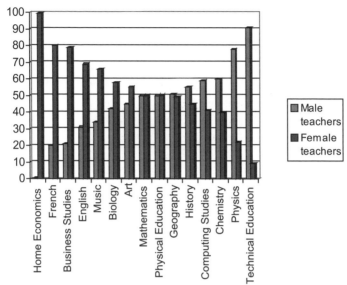

Figure 2.5: Secondary school teachers: main subject taught by gender, 2003 (percentages) (Scottish Executive, 2004)

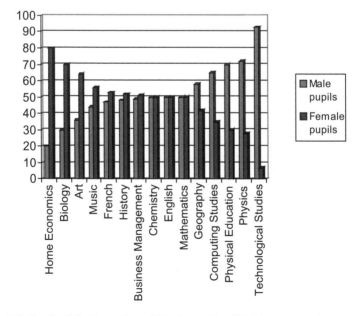

Figure 2.6: Standard Grade entries: subject by gender, 2005 (percentages) (Scottish Qualification Authority, 2006)

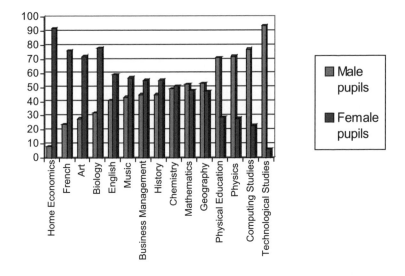

Figure 2.7: Higher Grade entries: subject by gender, 2005 (percentages)
(Scottish Qualification Authority, 2006)

Teachers, gender and the curriculum

Examining the distribution of teachers by age group and subject provides
fascinating insights into the gendered nature of particular subjects in the
future. The following figures provide a more detailed breakdown of subject
taught by age and gender and are derived from the General Teaching
Council for Scotland (GTCS) Register of fully registered teachers. It should
be noted that:

- Figures only take account of fully registered teachers as at 31
  March 2004. Some of these teachers may be working in the independent sector.

- Figures presented are based on the first subject an individual is
  registered to teach. Where fully registered teachers are registered to teach in more than one subject area, only the first subject
  of registration is considered for the purposes of this analysis.
  Teachers may, of course, not be teaching this subject.

A number of important points arise. In some subjects (e.g. Mathematics,
Combined Sciences, History and Modern Studies), it is evident that women

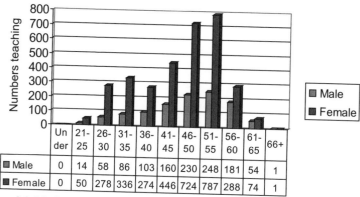

	Under	21-25	26-30	31-35	36-40	41-45	46-50	51-55	56-60	61-65	66+
■ Male	0	14	58	86	103	160	230	248	181	54	1
■ Female	0	50	278	336	274	446	724	787	288	74	1

Figure 2.8: Mathematics by age group and gender

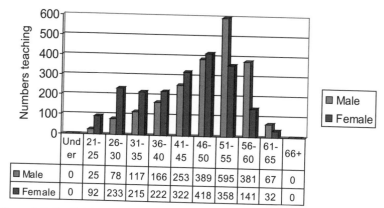

	Under	21-25	26-30	31-35	36-40	41-45	46-50	51-55	56-60	61-65	66+
■ Male	0	25	78	117	166	253	389	595	381	67	0
■ Female	0	92	233	215	222	322	418	358	141	32	0

Figure 2.9: English by age group and gender

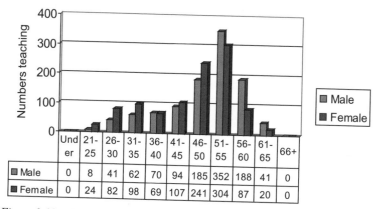

	Under	21-25	26-30	31-35	36-40	41-45	46-50	51-55	56-60	61-65	66+
■ Male	0	8	41	62	70	94	185	352	188	41	0
■ Female	0	24	82	98	69	107	241	304	87	20	0

Figure 2.10: All Sciences combined by age group and gender

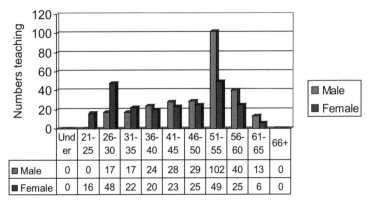

Figure 2.11: History by age group and gender

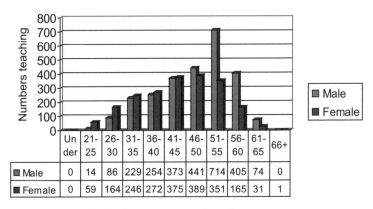

Figure 2.12: Modern Studies by age group and gender

predominate in the younger age groups whereas men predominate in the older age groups. In English, women have always been in the majority, but here too a change is evident since in the older age groups the gender imbalance in favour of women is less marked and, conversely, amongst younger recruits, the preponderance of women is even more evident. As a result of fewer men coming into teaching, there has been a significant change in the gender balance within many subject areas, and if future trends continue, subject departments which were traditionally male preserves will become female areas. On present showing, only highly polarised subjects such as Home Economics and Technological Studies will continue to be recognisable as 'male' or 'female' departments. Interesting questions arise with regard to the impact this will have on boys and girls in schools. If girls observe women teaching Physics and Chemistry, then it may be that natural science will cease to be regarded quite so strongly as a no-go area for future study and work. Clearly, boys too may have their assumptions about male and female knowledge domains challenged. Interestingly, although the proportion of boys studying Physics has remained virtually unchanged for the last twenty-five years, standing at about two-thirds of the total, the absolute number of pupils in this area has fallen, suggesting that the subject is becoming generally less attractive. Clearly, interesting questions arise with regard to the changing culture of the particular subjects in the light of the shifting gender balance of staff in the area, with attention being paid not only to the experiences of 'under-achieving' boys, but also to the experiences of girls, who have traditionally found few role models to emulate in particular areas of the curriculum.

Gender balance in teacher training

The gender balance of the teaching profession in the future is, of course, dependent on the characteristics of new recruits, so this section explores issues to do with entry to the profession. The number of students on the PGCE secondary, BEd primary and BEd secondary courses has been fairly stable between 1996 and 2003, with a small decline in the number of students on the BEd primary programme. The number of students on the PGCE primary programme has increased between 1996 and 2003, reflecting teacher supply needs.

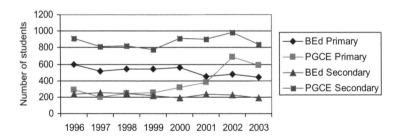

Figure 2.13: Students graduating from teacher training 1996–2003

Over the last three academic years, male graduates on the PGCE and BEd primary course have been fairly evenly spread across the 20-35+ age groups. However more women in their early 20s enrol on the programmes, indicating that primary school teaching is a first career choice, often applied for while studying for the undergraduate degree.

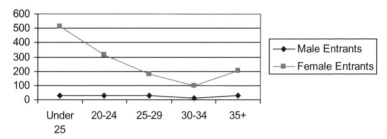

Figure 2.14: Primary PGCE and BEd students by age group and gender 2002/2003

By way of contrast, the majority of both male and female graduates entering the PGCE and BEd secondary education programmes are in the 20–24 age range, implying that graduates have enrolled for the course immediately after their first degree, or shortly thereafter.

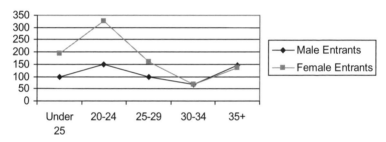

Figure 2.15: Secondary PGCE and BEd students by age group and gender 2002/2003

The main subject of PGCE entrants largely reflects the gendered pattern of subjects taught in school. However there are some differences, for example the number of male PGCE students training to teach History, Geography, Biology, Chemistry, Music and Technical Education is well below the percentage of male teachers currently teaching these subjects. The only subject which has a higher percentage of male students compared with existing male teachers is Business Studies as Table 2.3 shows.

Summary and conclusion

Analysis of Scottish Executive statistics demonstrates the fairly sharp drop in the proportion of men teaching in Scottish public sector schools. Men made up about a third of the teaching workforce in Scotland in 1994, but by 2003 this had fallen to only a quarter. The gap in the proportion of men and women in secondary school teaching is widening quite rapidly, whereas

Table 2.3: PGCE secondary graduates by gender and subject 2002-2003

Subject	Male graduates		Female graduates		Total
Biology	10	22%	35	78%	45
Business Studies	10	33%	20	67%	30
Chemistry	10	40%	15	60%	25
Computing Studies	25	56%	20	44%	45
English	25	24%	80	76%	105
French	5	14%	30	86%	35
Geography	15	43%	20	57%	35
History	15	38%	25	63%	40
Home Economics	0	0%	15	100%	15
Mathematics	35	47%	40	53%	75
Modern studies	15	43%	20	57%	35
Music	5	25%	15	75%	20
Physical Education	5	50%	5	50%	10
Physics	25	71%	10	29%	35
Technical Education	35	78%	10	22%	45
Total	235	39%	360	61%	**595**

Source: Higher Education Statistics Agency

the gender gap in primary is fairly static. The shortfall in male recruitment is currently being made up by an increase in female recruitment, and the reasons for women's continued attraction to teaching, compared with an evident lack of male interest, is one of the puzzling issues we consider in Chapters 3, 4 and 5.

The teaching workforce of Scottish schools is not only becoming more female, but is also ageing, with the majority of teachers aged over 44 in 2003. It is also fairly unreflective of ethnic diversity; all head teachers and deputes of secondary schools and head teachers of primary schools who declared their ethnicity described themselves as white–UK or white–other. Whilst the proportion of teachers from minority ethnic background is not out of kilter with their representation in the Scottish population more widely, there is a clear under-representation at senior levels. Furthermore, given the growing number of minority ethnic people in Scotland, there is a need for the teaching profession to reflect these wider social changes. Management in Scottish education is not only exclusively white, but is also heavily male-dominated, with men having much better chances of promotion in both primary and secondary schools. This may change in the near future, since about two thirds of candidates in the Standard for Headship in Scotland are now women.

In Scottish secondary schools in 2003 there was a traditional gender divide in subject taught, with men making up the majority of teachers in Chemistry, Physics, Geography, History, Computing Studies and Technical Education. However, an analysis by age, gender and subject taught suggests that this picture is about to change radically, since women in the younger age groups make up the majority of teachers in Mathematics, Science, History and Modern Studies. Younger female teachers also represent a higher proportion of English teachers. This may have implications for the culture of particular subject areas. For example, if girls observe that women make up the majority of teachers of a subject like Physics, traditionally dominated by men, there is a possibility that the subject will appear more attractive and their numbers will increase. If so, then the shifting gender balance of teachers might accomplish what decades of the promotion of science to girls failed to achieve. An entirely counter-productive outcome, of course, would be if both girls and boys were to vote against Physics with their feet, thus sabotaging the need for young scientists in the knowledge economy of the future.

Study of the composition of the student body in teacher training does not hold out much hope of a resurgence in the number of male recruits to teaching in the near future. On the PGCE primary programme, the majority of women are under 24 whilst men are more evenly spread across the 20–35 age groups. This suggests that for women primary teaching is a first career choice, whereas men are more likely to enter primary teaching having tried out other jobs. Amongst secondary PGCE students, the largest numbers are in the 20–24 age group, with another peak at age 35+. By far the largest group of PGCE secondary students are women in the 20–24 age group, suggesting that teaching is still a popular career choice for women after completing their first degree.

The main subject of students on the BEd and PGCE programmes reflects the gender balance in the wider teaching profession. However, the proportion of students training to teach History, Geography, Chemistry, Music and Technical Education is well below the proportion of men currently teaching these subjects in schools, indicating that the current trend towards an entire reshaping of the gender profile of subject departments will continue at least for the foreseeable future.

Clearly, different interpretations of these gendered patterns are possible. Hakim (2004), would argue that women have always been attracted to primary teaching because the majority have either a family-centred or adaptive/ drifter work orientation. Primary teaching, she would argue, fits women's individual preferences very well because of its associations with caring and because working hours fit reasonably well with family life. Secondary school teaching, Hakim's theory would suggest, whilst having reasonably family-friendly hours, would traditionally have been more attractive to adaptive and work-centred men because of its subject focus. However, it has been argued that secondary school teaching is becoming more concerned with caring and nurturing aspects, which might make it less attractive to men. Hakim would also suggest that the predominance of men in promoted posts would similarly reflect men's greater work orientation and desire for promotion. Discrimination within the workplace, or the active mentoring of men, would feature little in Hakim's explanation of work-based inequality. Whilst Crompton (2006) would broadly concur with Hakim's analysis of women's varying work orientations, she would disagree with Hakim in her emphasis on individual choice. Rather, she would argue, the assumption that women are innately suited to caring is an ideological construction serving the interests of both patriarchy and capitalism. Furthermore, the idea that women in particular have to adopt flexible working lives accords well with the new demands of flexible capitalism, and is promoted discursively rather than being simply a function of women's individual choices. These ideas are examined further through the lens of our survey with undergraduate students and discussions with practising teachers and key informants.

Chapter 3

UNDERGRADUATES' VIEWS OF
TEACHING AS A CAREER

Joanna Ferrie, Sheila Riddell and Anne Stafford

Introduction

University students' views provide a means of gaining insight into the reasons underlying the shifting gender balance in teaching and the extent to which present trends described in Chapter 2 are likely to continue into the future. We therefore conducted a survey of undergraduates in three Scottish universities in different parts of the country to investigate attitudes to future employment and, more specifically, perceptions of teaching. The institutions varied in relation to their history and social composition of the student body. University 1 is a large pre-1992 university whose students come predominantly from fairly affluent backgrounds. It has a particularly high proportion of students from the independent sector. University 2, also a large pre-1992 university, has a more mixed student intake and a far higher proportion of local students from state schools. University 3, a post-1992 institution, has the highest proportion of students from socially disadvantaged backgrounds and its curriculum is closely geared to the needs of the local economy. The questionnaire was completed by a sample of third year social science and biological sciences students at a time when most would have begun to think about their future options, without having yet committed themselves to a particular career or postgraduate course. Students were asked to complete the survey at the beginning or end of a teaching session, although in one university some questionnaires were completed online. A total of 323 questionnaires were returned, a 90 per cent response rate. This is, of course, very high for a survey of this type, and was due to the fact that in most cases the researchers waited in the lecture theatre whilst the students completed the questionnaire, collecting them individually as the students left.

Characteristics of the sample

Respondents were fairly evenly spread across the three universities, although there were more respondents from biological sciences compared with social sciences (see Tables 3.1 and 3.2).

Table 3.1: Number and percentage of respondents from the three universities

University	Number of respondents
University 1, pre-1992	93 (29%)
University 2, pre-1992	126 (39%)
University 3, post-1992	104 (32%)

There was no difference in the balance of males and females between the three universities.

Table 3.2: Number and percentage of respondents by course studies

Course	Number of respondents
Biology	171 (53%)
Sociology	125 (39%)
Sociology plus other	7 (2%)
Medicine	7 (2%)
Social Policy	12 (4%)

In order to obtain a measure of students' social background, deprivation category scores (DEPCAT) were generated from the home address postcodes, which were provided by roughly two-thirds of respondents. The Scottish Area Deprivation Index (Gibb *et al.*, 1998) measures the degree of area deprivation on a scale from 1 to 7, with 1 signifying the least deprived and 7 the most deprived areas. The areas are linked to current Scottish postcodes to allow easy application of the index. The Scottish Area Deprivation Index is based on six indicators most strongly associated with neighbourhood deprivation. These are the number of income support claimants; employment rate; households living below occupancy norm; index of home contents insurance company premia; non higher education participation and standardised mortality rates. Respondents were specifically asked for the postcode of their home address, rather than their term-time address. The results are illustrated graphically in Figure 3.1. As noted above, respondents with a DEPCAT score of 1 reside in the least deprived areas of Scotland, and those with a score of 7 reside in the most deprived.

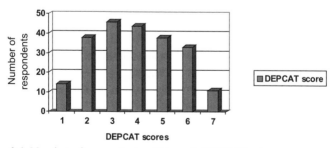

Figure 3.1: Number of respondents within each DEPCAT category

Although DEPCAT score did not appear to have a significant impact on whether respondents were likely to consider a career in education, according to chi-square, an interesting pattern did appear.

There was an interesting relationship between DEPCAT scores and university attended. It is evident that the students from Universities 1 and 2 were more socially advantaged than those from University 3, as Figure 3.2 illustrates.

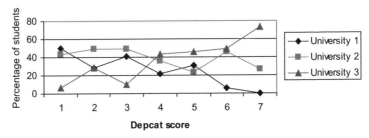

Figure 3.2: DEPCAT score of students' home postcode by university attended

As can be seen from the graph, most respondents in DEPCAT 1 attended University 1 (50 per cent) with slightly fewer attending University 2 (43 per cent), and far fewer attending University 3 (7 per cent). Most students in DEPCAT 7 attended University 3 (73 per cent), more than double the proportion attending University 2 (27 per cent), and there were no students at all in DEPCAT 7 attending University 1 (0 per cent).

Ages ranged from 19 to 52 with an expected majority clustering around the 20–21 year mark. There were almost twice as many female (n=206, 66 per cent) as male respondents (n=108, 34 per cent), but there was no relationship between gender and university attended.

Fourteen respondents (4 per cent) reported that they were disabled, and 12 were claiming Disabled Students Allowance (DSA) (4 per cent). There was no significant difference in the number of respondents who were disabled according to gender, but male respondents (9 per cent) were more likely than female students (1 per cent) to be claiming DSA. There was no relationship between disability and having considered teaching as a career.

Most respondents described their ethnicity as white–UK (86 per cent, n=275), and there was no relationship between ethnicity and gender or ethnicity and university attended. In addition, there was no association between ethnicity and considering a career in teaching.

Students' attitudes towards future employment

Students were asked to respond to a number of statements relating to career decision on a three-point scale (agree, neutral, disagree). The statements were:

- I want to have a job which will pay a high salary.
- I want a job which offers family-friendly conditions.
- I want a job which offers security and a steady income.
- I want a job with long holidays.
- I want a job which is socially useful.
- I want a job where I work with people.
- I want a job with high social status.
- I want a job which uses my degree.
- I want a job which will inspire future generations.

Figure 3.3 summarises the responses to the questions and Figure 3.4 illustrates male and female responses.

A striking feature of men's and women's responses is the overall similarity in their rating of the importance of a number of factors. So, for example, there is little difference between men's and women's views of the importance of having a secure and steady income, a socially useful job, a job which inspires others and a job which uses knowledge and skills acquired in a degree. A further striking feature is that students place greater weight on having a secure and steady income compared with having a highly paid job. Only about a third of students believe that having a job which brings high social status is very important, although there is a significant gender difference here, with men seeing social status as important. Perhaps surprisingly, only just over a half think that having a job which inspires others is important.

As noted above, the importance of a job with high social status is significantly more important to men than women, with 41 per cent of men agreeing with this statement as opposed to 27 per cent of women. Men also regard having a highly paid job as more important than women (73 per cent as opposed to 69 per cent). There is also a difference in men's and women's views of the importance of having a job which suits family life, which is seen as more important by women (66 per cent) than men (56 per cent). Most of these gender differences, however, were not statistically significant.

These findings perhaps indicate that even before starting their working lives, women are already operating with the expectation that they will make a contribution to the total family income, rather than seeing themselves as the main or as an equal breadwinner. Men, on the other hand, from a relatively early point are expressing attitudes which are consistent with a more strongly work-centred view of the world. Having said this, men's work orientation does not extend to a desire to sacrifice holidays; 56 per cent of men compared with 48 per cent of women felt that having a job with good holidays would be an advantage.

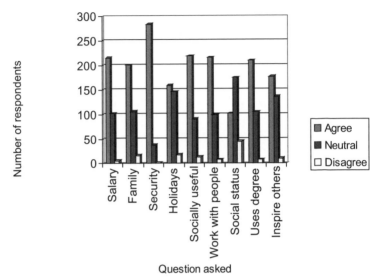

Figure 3.3: Responses to statements about career decisions

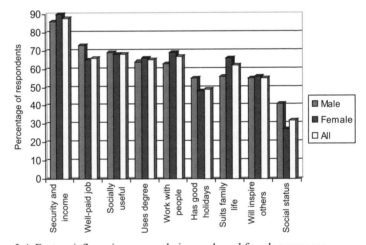

Figure 3.4: Factors influencing career choice: male and female responses

Preferred career options

Respondents were asked to indicate their chosen area of work, and were invited to give a first choice and a second choice. The most frequent answers are provided in Table 3.3.

Table 3.3: Number and percentage of respondents who selected first and second career choices

Profession/Response	First choice	Second choice
Scientific research	83 (25%)	39 (13%)
Teaching	32 (10%)	37 (12%)
Civil service	14 (4%)	9 (3%)
Conservation	13 (4%)	3 (1%)
Social work	12 (4%)	8 (3%)
Sociological research	10 (3%)	9 (4%)
Pharmaceutical industry	8 (3%)	---
Medical doctor	8 (3%)	---
Journalism	8 (3%)	7 (2%)
Higher education	7 (2%)	6 (2%)
Banking	5 (2%)	---
Nursing	5 (2%)	1 (0.3%)
Forensic Science	5 (2%)	---
Police Force	2 (1%)	15 (5%)
No response/don't know	60 (19%)	132 (41%)

As can be seen, most respondents had some idea about what kind of job they would like, though many did not have a second choice. Teaching was a relatively popular option, with over 20 per cent including it as a first or second choice option. Further to this, 193 respondents (60 per cent) said that they had considered a job in teaching, though presumably about 40 per cent had re-considered, or at least did not specify it as a first or second choice.

Particular views of teaching as a career

To probe attitudes to teaching further, respondents were asked to make an agree/neutral/disagree judgement concerning the following nine statements relating to teaching:

- Teaching is a reasonably well-paid job.
- Problems with classroom discipline make teaching an unpopular career choice.
- Teaching is a good job for people with family responsibilities.
- Teachers command a lot of public respect.
- There are good career prospects for teachers.
- Teachers' holidays make it an attractive career.
- Primary teaching is a more attractive career option than secondary teaching.
- I currently have experience of teaching.
- It is highly likely I will become a teacher.

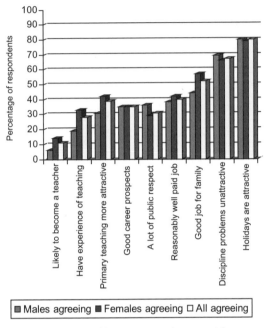

Figure 3.5: Level of agreement with statements about teaching as a career

As with general attitudes to future jobs, there were strong similarities between men and women in their views of teaching as a career, and overall the view of teaching was not particularly rosy. It appeared that for both men and women, the most positive feature of teaching was the long holidays, with 80 per cent agreement that this was an attractive aspect. Just over a third felt that teaching was a reasonably well-paid job and about a third felt that it offered good career prospects and commanded a lot of public respect. Two-thirds of both men and women believed that discipline problems made teaching an unattractive option.

There were some interesting differences between male and female responses, with a significantly higher proportion of women expressing the view that teaching was a good job for people with family responsibilities and a much higher proportion of women having had some experience of teaching (33 per cent of women as opposed to 19 per cent of men). Female respondents (42 per cent) were more likely than males (31 per cent) to agree with the statement 'Primary teaching is a more attractive career option than secondary teaching', though the difference was not statistically significant. Tellingly, more than twice as many women as men said that they were likely to become a teacher (14 per cent of women as opposed to 6 per cent of men)

Characteristics of those considering a job in teaching

Because of the particular focus of the research, we decided to look more closely at the characteristics of prospective teachers. Respondents were asked to make a yes/no judgement about whether they had considered teaching. Sixty perc ent (n=193) said they had considered a job in teaching and 40 per cent (n=130) had not, with a similar proportion of male and female respondents saying that they had looked at teaching as a possible future career option. This is considerably higher than the proportion of men and women who actually enrol on teacher training courses and finally enter the profession (see Chapter 2). There was no association between university attended and considering a career in teaching. However, some interesting differences emerged in relation to students' deprivation category as measured by their home postcode.

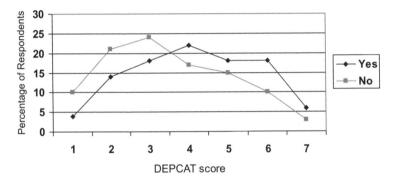

Figure 3.6: Have you considered a career in teaching? Question response explored using DEPCAT scores

As can be seen from Figure 3.6, respondents from DEPCAT areas 1–3, the least deprived, are less likely to have considered a career in teaching and, conversely, those living in DEPCAT areas 4–7, are more likely to have considered education as a career. Students with a DEPCAT score of 4 appeared to be the group who were most likely to consider becoming a teacher. In addition, students from more disadvantaged areas were significantly more likely to agree with the statement 'Teaching is a reasonably well-paid job.' Figure 3.7 illustrates this pattern.

Those who were considering teaching as a career appeared to have significantly different attitudes to their future working lives on a number of dimensions. For example, a job offering family-friendly conditions was significantly more important to this group compared with those who were not considering teaching. Those who had considered a career in education were also significantly more likely to believe that long holidays were important,

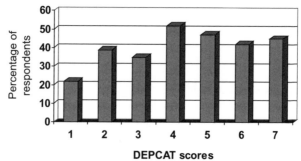

Figure 3.7: Percentage of respondents in agreement with the statement 'Teaching is a reasonably well-paid job', by DEPCAT scores

Table 3.4: Attitudes of those considering or not considering a career in teaching

	Agreement by those considering teaching career	Agreement by those NOT considering teaching career
Want job with family-friendly conditions	67%	55%
Long holidays important	52%	45%
Teachers' holidays make it an attractive career	82%	75%
Want job with high social status	26%	39%
Want job working with other people	70%	62%
Teaching is reasonably well paid job	47%	30%
Teaching is a good job for people with family responsibilities	58%	44%
Have work experience in teaching	35%	15%
Problems with discipline make teaching an unpopular career choice	62%	72%
Teachers command a lot of public respect	27%	36%
Highly likely I will become a teacher	16%	4%

and to agree with the statement 'Teachers' holidays make it an attractive career', compared with those that had not considered a teaching career. In addition, people considering a job in teaching were more likely to agree with the statement 'I want a job where I work with other people' and were significantly less likely to agree with the statement, 'I want a job with high social status'. As might be expected, those that had considered a career in teaching were more likely to agree with the statement 'Teaching is a reasonably well-paid job', and were significantly more likely to agree with the statement 'Teaching is a good job for people with family responsibilities.' As expected, respondents who had considered a career in teaching were significantly more likely to have work experience in the area.

Respondents who had considered a career in education were less likely to agree with the statement 'Problems with classroom discipline make teaching an unpopular career choice' and, perhaps surprisingly, were also less likely to agree with the statement 'Teachers command a lot of public respect' than those who were not thinking of becoming a teacher.

Variations in response between students at different universities

Some interesting differences emerged between students at different universities, reflecting to some extent the composition of the student body. Overall, students at University 3, a new university with a socially mixed intake, tended to be more instrumental in their attitudes to future employment than students at the pre-1992 universities. As can be seen from Figure 3.9, a higher percentage of students attending University 3 (80 per cent) agreed with the statement 'I want to have a job which will pay a high salary' compared with students from University 1 (68 per cent) and University 2 (55 per cent).

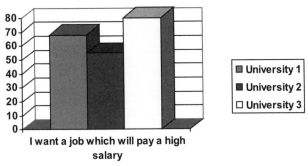

Figure 3.8: Percentage of respondents in agreement with the statement 'I want a job which will pay a high salary', from University 1, University 2 and University 3

Again respondents from University 3 were significantly more likely to support the idea of having a job with high social status.

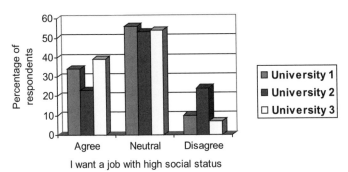

Figure 3.9: Percentage of respondents agreeing with the statement 'I want a job with high social status', by university attended

Respondents from University 3 (59 per cent) were more likely than students from University 2 (46 per cent) and University 1 (43 per cent) to agree with the statement 'I want a job with long holidays.' They were also significantly more likely to feel that they wanted a job which involved working with other people compared with students at the other two universities.

There were some indications that students at University 3 had a more positive attitude toward teaching as a career. For example, 50 per cent agreed with the statement 'Teaching is a reasonably well-paid job', compared with 41 per cent of respondents from University 2 and 27 per cent of respondents at University 1. This reflects the possibility that students at universities with different social profiles differ with regard to what they consider to be a well-paid. As noted earlier, University 3 students are from a more diverse range of backgrounds, and therefore teaching might appear to them to be a relatively well-paid job in the light of their expectations. Students from more advantaged backgrounds at Universities 1 and 2 may have higher expectations of what constitutes a well-paid job.

Table 3.5: Agreement with the statement 'Teaching is a reasonably well-paid job' by university

	Agree	Neutral	**Disagree**
University 1	25 (27%)	38 (41%)	30 (32%)
University 2	52 (41%)	43 (34%)	31 (25%)
University 3	52 (50%)	35 (36%)	12 (11%)

Summary and conclusions

In the following section, we summarise questionnaire findings and draw out some of the key differences. On the face of it, many of the views expressed by respondents appeared to be compatible with opting for a career in teaching. For example, job security and a steady income were rated highly and about two-thirds thought that a job that suited family life was important. About half the sample, and more men than women, thought that having good holidays would influence their career choice. Less than a third felt that high social status was important. These general attitudes appear to be compatible with opting for teaching as a career.

Having said this, students had a rather negative view of teaching as a career. Two- thirds said they wanted a highly paid job and only 40 per cent thought that teaching fell into this category. Only a third believed that teaching offered good promotion prospects, and commanded public respect, and counter-intuitively, people who had considered a career in teaching were more likely than others to regard it as having low social status. More than two-thirds thought that discipline problems made it an unpopular career choice.

Whereas 60 per cent of respondents had considered a job in teaching, the majority appeared to have rejected this option, with only 11 per cent saying they were very likely to become a teacher. Good holidays and family-friendly conditions of service appeared to have positively influenced such decisions.

Men and women generally agreed in their judgements about the factors affecting career decisions and in their assessment of teaching as a career. Women were significantly more likely than men to see teaching as a good job for people with family responsibilities. More women than men thought that primary teaching was more attractive than secondary teaching, had experience of teaching and thought they were likely to become a teacher, although none of these differences was statistically significant.

People considering a career in teaching had a more rosy view of the job than others and placed higher value on family-friendly conditions, long holidays and working with people, and less importance on having a job with high social status. They were less likely to believe that problems with discipline made teaching an unattractive option.

Some fascinating associations emerged between student social background and attitudes to teaching. Those from less advantaged backgrounds were more likely to be considering teaching as a career and to regard it as a reasonably well-paid job. There were no differences by university, indicating that students from less advantaged areas, regardless of which university they attended, shared these views. This pattern fits with suggestions from the literature (e.g. Kay 2001), which indicate that middle-class women have moved into certain professional occupations such as law and medicine, whilst undergraduates from poorer backgrounds continue to pursue careers in traditionally female professions such as teaching.

Undergraduates from the post-1992 university, with more diverse social backgrounds, were significantly more likely than those from the pre-1992 universities to regard a high salary, high social status and long holidays as important. They were also more likely to think that teaching was a reasonably well-paid job.

Overall, it appears that women and those from less advantaged neighbourhoods see teaching as a possible career, although perhaps for different reasons. For women, teaching appears to appeal to those who are looking for a family-friendly career, whilst recognising that compared with other jobs there may be disadvantages such as poorer pay, career prospects and social status. For students from more socially disadvantaged backgrounds, teaching may offer the possibility of social mobility, and this is supported by their desire for a well-paid job with high social status, and their perception that teaching may in fact offer reasonable pay and conditions.

As noted earlier, there is agreement among sociologists of employment that men and women differ in their career orientation, with men more focused on the work-centred end of the spectrum and women tending towards the adaptive and family-centred end. Disagreements focus on the extent to which this reflects individual or socially structured choices, and the extent to which such orientations are stable or shifting over the course of an individual's life. Findings of the undergraduate survey support the suggestion that those attracted to teaching have less of a work-centred orientation, and are more concerned about a range of other factors broadly relating to work–life balance.

Chapter 4

PROMOTING TEACHING AS A CAREER:
THE VIEWS OF UNIVERSITY CAREERS OFFICERS
AND KEY INFORMANTS

Anne Stafford and Lyn Tett

Introduction

We suggested in Chapter 1 that one influence on the decision by men and women to enter the teaching profession was the careers advice they received, so in this chapter we report on the views of three people working in three different University Careers Services who were interviewed about the reasons underlying the choice of teaching as a career. We also asked them to comment on the growing imbalance between men and women in the profession and to suggest some positive actions to promote teaching to students. The other people with an interest in promoting teaching as a career are those who are involved in training, supporting and employing teachers and so we interviewed staff from a range of positions as detailed in Table 4.1 below.

Table 4.1: Key informants: interviews conducted

Gender	**Role**
1 Male, 1 Female	Co-ordinators, Primary PGCE ITE programmes in 2 universities
Female	Co-ordinator, Secondary ITE programme
Male	University Dean of Faculty of Education
2 Females	Co-ordinators, BEd ITE programmes in 2 universities
Male	Local authority director of education
Male	Scottish Executive
2 Male, 1 Female	Secondary head teachers
2 Female	Primary head teachers
Female	GTCS
Female	Educational Institute of Scotland (EIS)
Female	HMIE

These key informants were interviewed about their views of teaching as a career; balance of women and men in teaching; distribution of women and men in different sectors; specific factors affecting male recruitment; promotion opportunities; possibilities for positive action. In this chapter we consider firstly the views of careers officers and then those of our key informants in relation to the issues of promoting teaching as a career.

Careers officers' views

Factors influencing graduate career choices

Careers officers suggested that most students wanted a job that enabled them to continue using their degree and were also likely to be interested in the idea of doing something useful or putting something back into society and this applied equally to men and women. Science graduates, the majority of whom are men, were more likely to want a career in science with less idea about alternative career opportunities. Social science graduates tended to be clearer and more articulate about career choices and alternative ways to use their degree. It was considered that women might slightly favour a career affording a better work–life balance. One careers officer suggested that mature students were particularly likely to favour a career which would allow them to remain in Scotland and for this reason teaching might be seen as an obvious profession to choose. It was suggested that students opting for the Post Graduate Certificate in Education (PGCE) fell into two groups, those who had always wanted to teach and those who saw teaching as a last resort. Men were more likely to fall into the latter group and were generally less strongly motivated.

Careers staff speculated that men might find it difficult to imagine themselves as teachers as a result of having had less interaction with children. It was felt that when male students come to interview, this lack of experience of working with children might count against them. The requirement for police checks on volunteers might make it more difficult for potential applicants to teacher education courses to organise a work experience placement at short notice. This would of course affect women and men equally, but young men might not have regarded teaching as a long-term career goal and therefore might have accumulated less work experience with children in informal settings. Female applicants, on the other hand, were more likely than men to have had prior experience of working with children, for example, helping out at Brownies or babysitting. Once on the course, male students might find it difficult to cope with a largely female environment, particularly those training to teach in the primary sector.

Specific views of teaching

Careers officers believed that interest in teaching as a career had declined over the years, and men in particular were less keen to enter the profession.

They noted that one reason for this might be the pull factor of other more attractive job opportunities in information technology and the electronics industry. However, they did not believe that this was the main reason for the falling numbers of men in teaching, since these jobs were in short supply and 'the graduate labour market in Scotland is not healthy'. Rather than embarking on a teaching career, they suggested that many graduates were working in call centres and supermarkets, and were thus under-employed.

A more likely reason was that it was now widely understood by students that teaching was a difficult and demanding job and that most teachers were working beyond their contracted hours. Despite this there was still a feeling that the terms and conditions were a positive feature, particularly job security, and that these factors might be more attractive to women than men because of their family-friendly nature. Views on the effect of salary on recruitment varied. One officer claimed that students were now aware that the salary was now 'decent' and this was a hopeful development. If graduates were not choosing teaching as a career, it was not because of the money. Another questioned whether awareness of the recent pay increase had filtered down to students, and there was also a possible lack of awareness of the teacher induction scheme. On the other hand it was suggested that at least some students were aware of these changes and had been attracted to teaching as a result.

On the negative side, careers staff felt that male students might view teaching as a female occupation and therefore not a job for men.

> Sometimes I think primary teaching is still seen as a bit soft by men. Men are supposed to be men and they are still supposed to be tough and things like that and teaching is not a real man's job.

It was also argued that the new emphasis on inclusion might contribute to the image of teaching as women's work and might be off-putting to men.

> . . . the amount of stuff that keeps getting piled onto schools, where teachers would appear to be responsible for almost everything down to teaching kids to blow their nose. That kind of stuff does not attract men. They might want to teach their subject and be academic about it. Men are somehow less interested in the altruistic side, the pastoral care part, the development of good citizens of the future . . .

Careers staff also felt that teaching received a generally bad press that was likely to deter new recruits:

> I think sometimes when you see these kinds of things on Reporting Scotland or reading the *Herald* or the *Scotsman* or whatever, it is terribly easy to get an awful negative image of what is actually happening in this profession. Lawyers come in for a bad press sometimes but not in the same way as teachers are getting it in the neck.

Teachers were also implicated in promoting a negative view of their profession. Students reported conversations with practising teachers, sometimes family members, who had advised them against a career in education. Careers staff believed that most students who were considering teaching had not thought much beyond working with and inspiring young people. Promotion opportunities were not seen as a major consideration at this stage, although the thought of promotion might be more attractive to men 'because women may be more altruistic and men more clinical'. A second careers adviser said that a few high flying students might see opportunities for promotion as a factor in choosing teaching.

Promoting teaching as a career
Careers staff did not favour action directed solely at men, since targeting particular groups, such as minority ethnic students, had turned out in the past to be ineffective:

> Our feedback here is that whenever we try to advertise events that are targeted at ethnic minority students, the police service do it, government does it, the feedback we get is they don't want to be different.

They believed that generally promoting teaching positively as a serious profession would attract better graduates in general and this would include more men. Careers service respondents did not think they could do more to promote teaching, since their remit was to give impartial guidance.

However, the public sector might be able to learn lessons from commercial bodies, many of whom placed a high premium on the effective marketing of their organisations to university careers services and students in order to recruit the best labour force. Careers officers were in regular touch and on first name terms with graduate recruiters in commercial organisations such as Proctor and Gamble, Unilever and Price Waterhouse Coopers. These companies regularly informed the university careers services of upcoming vacancies, gave presentations to students and attended recruitment fairs. They were very strategic and saw the university careers service as important.

Public bodies, by way of contrast, were less strategic. They generally did not make personal contact with university careers officers and therefore failed to use the services to best effect:

> I would have to say that anything to do with public sector careers, their recruitment strategies are mediocre by comparison with commercial organisations.

Suggestions to those responsible for teacher recruitment, principally the Scottish Executive and local authorities, included building better relationships with university careers services, speaking directly to groups of students and producing better publicity material about teaching as a career

They also mentioned that websites about teaching as a career needed to be more user-friendly. One suggestion was that the website should include video clips of teachers in the classroom and case study material designed to engage students' interest. There was also 'a job to be done to persuade teachers themselves to be positive about their profession'.

Key informants' views

Underlying reasons for the declining proportion of men in teaching

Key informants were asked why they thought there had been a decline in the proportion of men entering and staying in the profession. Many suggested that the more women there are in a profession, the less attractive it is to men. For example, a secondary head suggested that:

> Kids in school, for example, see a female doing a job and associate that with only that gender.

A primary head suggested that:

> Society is becoming more gender stereotyped again and men are less likely to cross the traditional gender roles.

Others suggested that in a healthy labour market, men were more likely to choose one of the 'new' occupations, which were seen as more exciting and adventurous.

Many key informants thought that the reasons for the declining proportion of men in teaching varied by sector. The primary sector, it was believed, had always been regarded as a women's profession because it was seen as being about 'caring', and therefore the natural domain of women rather than men. As a result of this association, primary schools had historically been the Cinderella sector, with lower pay, qualifications and status. The HMIE representative suggested that 'Women are interested in the things children do', whereas men were much more subject orientated. A number of key informants suggested that there were more limited career prospects in primary and that this deterred men from applying. For example the co-ordinator of a primary ITE programme suggested that the growth of women in senior management, particularly in primary schools, made men feel a little less secure about their own rise through the ranks.

A primary head suggested that:

> Teaching is seen as being about 'caring', especially in the early years, so this is not attractive to men. Society is also wary about males – it's seen as not a job for a 'real' man, especially by parents. For example, last year I had a man in his fifties in the nursery who I appointed for six months maternity cover and one of the parents phoned me to tell me there was a paedophile in the classroom because she'd seen him through the window after hours.

This was a clear example of the way in which the options available to men and women are limited by public perceptions. As the HMIE representative pointed out:

> . . . one of the things we do need to be careful about is . . . because of issues around protecting children, we don't build a culture that makes it difficult for men to be involved in childcare and early years work.

In the secondary sector it was suggested by the ITE co-ordinators that in the male-dominated subject areas such as Physics and Computer Science there were better financial prospects in industry. In addition, the bad press about indiscipline and other difficulties in this sector was likely to put people off from applying:

> The best way to recruit people would be if people stopped going on about how hard it is all the time. (HMIE)

Many suggested that men seek higher earning occupations than teaching although it appeared that the general public were not aware of the recent changes in the salary structure following the McCrone Agreement. Part of this perception was due to the loss of recognition of the profession in the 1980s and 1990s coupled with the relatively poor salaries at that time, the secondary heads suggested. These factors made men less likely to enter teaching in the first place and those that did were more likely to leave for a better-paid job. It was argued that, as people's worth is increasingly measured in financial terms, then that becomes the most important criterion for getting and keeping a job. Another suggested reason was 'a move away from the emphasis on subject specific teaching [towards] a greater emphasis on the child' (EIS representative). The co-ordinator of a secondary teacher education course said that for men considering a change of job there was a disincentive to join the profession as there was 'no longer any recognition of their mature status in terms of starting salary and beyond'. This had a particular impact on men as mature women joining the profession were much more likely to have had a career break and therefore did not have to make such a financial sacrifice.

Consequences of fewer men entering the profession

Key informants were asked if they thought it was a problem that fewer men are going into teaching. Most thought it was, mainly because they felt that men provided good role models for boys, many of whom had negative experiences of the men in their lives. The growth of single female-headed households made it even more important for boys to be taught by men, at least for part of their primary education. As one director of education pointed out:

In some primary schools there are no men at all. Not even the janitor and that is not a good idea.

An ITE co-ordinator said:

There are wee children clinging to the male student's legs because they just don't see men in their lives.

The ideal situation, it was suggested by all the head teachers, was a balance so both sexes have role models and this challenged residual stereotypes about the roles of men and women in society. Having men in teaching also has the potential to challenge people's ideas about masculinity, which is particularly important for young men:

Children need to see male role models that are both supportive and challenging. So they need to see men in a caring and dynamic role just like girls in the past needed to see women in a dynamic role because they only saw women in a caring role. Young people need to see both these qualities modelled by both sexes. (secondary head)

A primary head also suggested that a mixed staff group generated a 'gender inter-relationship that is very good for staff'.

Several key informants were concerned about stereotyping the contributions that males and females make to society through education. They argued that the main concern should be recruiting the best person to do the job, so in some ways the person's sex was of secondary importance. One suggested:

I think that men and women have an equal contribution to make towards young people and the development of our future society in all ways and it is important that both have a contribution to make. (ITE co-ordinator).

Another suggested that the idea of reproducing the structure of the traditional nuclear family might be admirable but was actually out-moded, since a decreasing number of people lived in families of this type:

If you are in a co-educational school and the balance of the school is about 50:50, then in terms of what impact you would like to have, you would like that to be 50:50 in terms of the school maybe taking the place of the family home. However, the reality in our society today is that is not the case. A lot of children come from single parent homes where the mother is the main person they are staying with. (secondary head)

Some key informants including the HMIE representative, the EIS representative and the ITE co-ordinators considered that although there were reasons why there should be more males in schools, especially primary schools, the importance of gender balance had to be looked at in the wider societal context. For example, one ITE co-ordinator suggested that:

Women may be more open to being changed than men are . . . [so] maybe primary schools would be worse places if more men were in them.

Specific factors affecting male recruitment into teaching
Key informants were asked what they thought attracted people into teaching and if there were any factors that appealed more to either women or men. Most thought that people who had enjoyed their school experience were attracted into teaching so they could give children and young people a similarly positive experience. The most important factor was that people had a liking for children and young people and had a positive view of the challenges involved in working with them. Teachers should feel that they were playing a worthwhile social role and should enjoy seeing people learn. Many suggested that the key factors were a belief that an individual could make a difference and change things for the better. Some key informants suggested that in the secondary sector people come into teaching because of their love and enjoyment of their subject area. For example, one secondary ITE coordinator suggested that many 'come for a change of career because they don't feel that in other jobs their subject skills are being appreciated fully'.

Generally, all the reasons given above were seen as applying to men and women equally, but it was thought that some of the conditions of service might appeal more to women than men. Many suggested that, particularly for women with children, the long holidays and the set hours were attractive and it meant that they did not have to arrange childcare during school holidays. Head teachers pointed out, however, that the profession was very demanding and not at all family-friendly in the actual hours it was necessary to work to be an effective teacher. Opportunities for promotion and a good pension were considered to be factors that might be more appealing to men than women. A few key informants knew of mature men who had moved from other careers attracted by the secure employment offered by the public sector after they had experienced redundancy in private sector occupations. The two primary heads suggested that the key factor was whether the person regarded themselves as the main breadwinner. Some couples now shared this role and increasingly women regarded their salary as a major rather than a constituent part of household income with themselves as the main breadwinner. A director of education suggested that 'gender is a spectrum rather than a divide' and that some women could be more aggressive and driven than some men in their approach to their careers and promotion.

Promotion and development opportunities
Key informants were asked why they thought women were less likely to become head teachers than men, particularly in the secondary sector. Many considered that the mismatch was mostly historical as there were more men

who entered secondary teaching in the 1970s and 1980s and they had progressed through the system. However, there was now a higher number of women at depute and principal teacher level so that in five to ten years time there would be equal numbers of male and female head teachers. It was suggested that there was a perception in the past that headships were not open to women but that an equal opportunities approach had changed that. Opportunities for mature women to return to the workforce meant that those who had missed opportunities at an earlier stage in their lives now had the chance to catch up.

On the other hand, it was acknowledged that women who had children often had to take career breaks and that the disruption of having a broken career pattern made promotion more difficult. Clearly, as a number of key informants pointed out, this pattern should not necessarily lead to less chances of promotion for women. One primary head suggested that:

> Women need to be better than men to get the same post because of the prejudice against them particularly from parents on the school board who are involved in appointment decisions.

A director of education concurred and suggested that school board members and councillors bring 'very old fashioned, often very patriarchal ideas' about the appropriate sex of a head teacher in both primary and secondary sectors. Several suggested that there were still significant sexist attitudes around that meant it was more likely that appointment panels would appoint men, especially in large secondary schools. Two ITE co-ordinators and the primary heads suggested that men were more likely to apply for promotion than women even if they might not yet have acquired the necessary experience. A primary head suggested that:

> Women are more likely to agonise over applying and not take risks. Men are also more likely to plan their careers and go for posts that will get them noticed whereas women don't care as much about promotion.

The HMIE representative thought that there were some men 'who come into teaching with the sole objective of becoming the head of a secondary school or a director of education'. On the other hand, the GTCS representative suggested that women were now applying for promotion in both the primary and secondary sectors and 'seeing it as a real option and not something they wouldn't aspire to so there has been a huge move'.

Key informants were also asked if they thought that the changes introduced into teaching by the McCrone settlement made it (a) a more attractive career in general (b) more appealing to either men or women.

Almost all our key informants considered that the increase in pay had made it a more attractive career but most doubted that this change had penetrated into the consciousness of the majority of the population who did not already have a connection with teaching. One ITE secondary co-ordinator pointed out, however, that the starting salary was good if you came in after graduation but not if you had given up a career to come into secondary teaching. Before the McCrone Agreement, mature entrants had started higher up the scale but now all had the same starting salary. Another more positive aspect of the McCrone Agreement was that it enabled more teachers to be given a pay increase and still stay in the classroom, particularly in the primary sector. It was considered that a number of teachers would prefer not to have to take on the demanding administrative tasks that were associated with the head teacher role. However, it was thought that this flatter career structure might be a disincentive to ambitious men particularly in the secondary sector. A number thought that the increased pay was more likely to appeal to men than women. The requirement to undertake CPD was considered positive, and might have the effect of encouraging women to take their careers more seriously. An ITE co-ordinator suggested that:

> The expectation of CPD [especially through the chartered teacher programme] will encourage more women [to go on to] seek promotion and that is a good thing.

Quality of new recruits

Key informants were asked what they thought about the general quality of people going into teaching. Nearly all were very positive and referred to the high quality of new recruits. A primary head suggested that current training has much greater depth and the 'level they are asked to perform at is good'. A secondary head said 'their abilities are far greater and they are far better prepared than we ever were'. The GTCS representative argued that 'the quality of the profession is higher than it has ever been'. Another, who was a co-ordinator of a BEd primary course, suggested that in terms of 'their academic qualifications it's much more rigorous and difficult'. It was felt that more people were going into the profession who really wanted to teach than had in the past and that some of the people who had been in the profession for some time were less able than the new entrants.

Many key informants, however, felt that male new entrants and applicants were less well qualified and motivated than females. Nearly all providers of ITE programmes considered that the quality of male applicants was less high than that of females. For example, one BEd primary co-ordinator suggested:

> The young men that apply don't seem to be as serious as the young women are. You can tell they are not going to get far in the interview because they are perceived as being immature, really not with knowledge of what is involved.

Another co-ordinator of the primary PGCE suggested that, although the quality of male applicants had been low in the past, he had 'seen a sea change in the quality of male candidates coming forward in the past few years'. It appears that the different types of programmes may attract a different quality of male applicants. All programme co-ordinators reported that they had looked carefully at their recruitment procedures to try to ensure that they were not discriminating against men but had found no evidence of bias.

In terms of entrants to the profession there was a clear message from some key informants that the quality of male recruits was lower than that of the females. One secondary head suggested that:

> For every job that I interview now, at any level, the overwhelming majority of candidates are women and the men tend to be, in general, the weaker candidates [because it is] the minority of them that are coming in positively with commitment.

No other respondent was quite as forthright as this, but many stressed the ability of the female entrants in particular. The GTCS representative reported that 'in secondary the vast majority that don't make [full registration] are older male entrants who are career changers'.

Positive actions

Key informants were asked if they thought that any positive actions should be taken to recruit more men into teaching. This was seen as a rather ambiguous question because as one, a director of education, put it 'frankly as a man, we have been advantaged for centuries and we can't just go back and revisit that because we have some worrying statistics'. The EIS representative pointed out that positive action implied that 'men and women . . . are two separate homogenous groups' whereas there are as 'many differences between women and women as between men and men'.

Several key informants were concerned that the vocational nature of teaching should not be compromised by targeting men simply because they were male since if 'it is easy to get in and they didn't succeed at something else you get recruits who become not very good teachers' (HMIE). Most key informants felt that the teaching workforce should reflect the population as a whole and therefore it was important that men were involved. However, it was equally important that other under-represented groups such as ethnic minorities and disabled people were recruited into the workforce. A primary head suggested:

> The more diverse the workforce, the better the experience that children have. This applies to all aspects including race, age, class and so on. I would like the staff in my school to reflect the community out there.

Another reason for encouraging more male entrants was so there were good role models for boys. As one secondary head argued 'if the boys don't see clever, dynamic, interesting but supportive men in front of them then they're not going to go into teaching'. It was also suggested that teaching should be promoted as something that is attractive to the whole population, not just a section of it: 'We do need general campaigns to make teaching more attractive' (HMIE). Several key informants pointed out that such campaigns should try to shift the negative media focus on discipline and also stress the positive aspects of teaching such as the pay structure and conditions of service.

Key informants offered a variety of specific suggestions that would encourage male recruitment. Several suggested that an advertising campaign promoting the pay and promotion opportunities that are now available to teachers would particularly attract men. A primary head teacher commented that 'no two days are ever the same' and felt that this variety was attractive to men who had already experienced either a boring or a very demanding job. 'Men come in … when they get disillusioned with very achievement focused type jobs' (HMIE). Similarly an advertising campaign that featured good male teachers, especially in the primary sector, was seen as important. An ITE co-ordinator and a primary head suggested that recruitment events in both the university sector and the local authorities that were led by men would be effective. Another issue raised was the need to think more about the retention of teachers, as it was the experience of one secondary head and of the GTCS representative that men were more likely to leave the profession than women.

It was suggested that early intervention in helping boys to see teaching as a possible option would be helpful. For example, boys should be encouraged to consider primary teaching whilst still at school, and might be helped to negotiate a primary school work placement. A primary head suggested that:

> Primary schools could promote greater awareness of gender stereotyping in jobs as part of the equalities agenda. The focus tends to be on race and disability generally because people see these as more of an issue. Gender isn't a 'fashionable' topic in schools partly because if you have an all female staff they just don't notice gender issues, just like white people aren't aware of racism as an issue for them.

All key informants were against positive discrimination for men either at the point of application for ITE or at entry, but argued that a culture should be created in education where 'both genders are equal and teaching is a career for all' (secondary ITE co-ordinator). The EIS representative and a director of education suggested that it was important to be clear about the role of gender in influencing educational outcomes relative to other factors:

The cause of a lot of boys' under attainment is related to economic position, deprivation, ethnicity, there are often multiple factors and I think there is too much generalization around about that whole business of gender. (director of education)

Summary and conclusion

In the view of the careers officers and key informants, individuals' gendered identities clearly impacted on their employment decisions. Both groups of respondents identified factors that were strongly associated with women's gendered identities and therefore might deter men from considering teaching as a career. One reason they considered that teaching was seen increasingly as a 'woman's job' was the association of education with 'caring'. This demanded 'soft' qualities, particularly in the primary sector and, in the secondary sector, the growing demands on teachers to assist with pupils' social development was also associated more with traditional views of women rather than men. These changes in teaching, particularly in the secondary sector, with a lesser emphasis on subject specific expertise, were seen as not fitting in with the gendered identities normally associated with men.

Another factor which might work against men applying to enter a teacher education programme was that courses generally expected candidates to have prior experience of working with children. Arranging work experience in schools now took longer and was more difficult because of the need for police checks and men did not have the same opportunities as women to work in other settings with children because of gendered assumptions about their identity. In addition men on teacher training courses might be uncomfortable in a predominantly female environment. So gender and employment appear to be strongly influenced by identity issues that operate both in relation to individual agency but are also affected by structural factors such as the gendered labour market.

The image of teaching as a system that was driven by performance management did not appear to have had an impact on recruitment in the view of our respondents. Careers officers commented that, compared with the private sector, the public sector appeared to put less energy into graduate recruitment. A more strategic approach to graduate recruitment would result in a better qualified and more enthusiastic teaching force. Positive aspects of teaching included the terms and conditions of employment which might be appreciated rather more by women than men, especially as women are more likely to favour careers offering a positive work–life balance.

Careers officers suggested that pay was not the major motivating factor in making decisions about employment. They considered that the generally negative image of teaching was more important. Mass media were partly responsible for the propagation of scare stories, but teachers themselves project an overwhelmingly negative view of their own profession, dampening the enthusiasm of new recruits. In addition there was a greater range of career options for men with qualifications in Maths, Science and Engineering.

The consequence of fewer men entering the profession was seen to be a problem, particularly in the primary sector due to the lack of role models for boys in the view of our key informants. They thought that pupils should have the experience of being taught by both men and women so that residual stereotypes could be challenged. A counter narrative, however, suggested that the importance of male role models could be overplayed and what actually mattered was ensuring that the best-qualified and motivated people entered the profession regardless of their sex.

These parallel narratives are important, since the former assumes the primacy of biological sex, whilst the latter problematises that view. Those arguing the case for increasing the number of men entering teaching maintain that an equal representation of men and women is the ideal. An alternative view is that the biological sex of the teacher is immaterial, since gender identity is not embodied, and what really matters is where teachers locate themselves on the gender spectrum, with the possibility of cross-over between men and women with regard to their social and emotional charac-teristics and work orientations.

Chapter 5

ADDRESSING THE GENDER BALANCE
IN TEACHING: PRACTISING TEACHERS' VIEWS

Alan Ducklin, Sheila Riddell, Anne Stafford,
Lyn Tett, Mandy Winterton

Introduction

In this chapter we report on our findings from practising teachers. Focus groups provided important insights into the way in which they made sense of their own decision to teach and their perceptions of the gendered nature of the profession as a whole. In the following sections we provide a brief description of each school and a summary of the main points made in the focus group discussions. There were some important contrasts between primary and secondary school focus groups and so we present findings from the secondary and primary school focus groups separately before drawing out key points. The location and number of participants in the groups is detailed in Table 5.1 below.

Table 5.1: Focus groups with teachers

School	Primary	Secondary
Northwalls Academy (Urban)		1 men's group (7)
		1 women's group (7)
Golflands High (Rural)		1 men's group (6)
		1 women's group (7)
Westside Primary (Urban)	1 mixed group	(2 men and 4 women)
Hilltop Primary (Rural)	1 mixed group	(2 men and 3 women)

Secondary school focus groups

Northwalls Academy: school background

The school is a large comprehensive in an urban area with more than a thousand pupils. Almost 50 per cent are from minority ethnic backgrounds and many different languages are spoken. The gender balance in the school is about 50:50, although among the younger age group women are in the majority. The school also employs a significant number of teachers from minority ethnic backgrounds. The school's catchment area is diverse, ranging from an area of multiple deprivation to more middle class areas on the outskirts of the city.

Golflands High: school background
The school is a large comprehensive in a small town serving a rural area with relatively low levels of deprivation. Apart from a small number of children who commute into a nearby city to attend independent schools, almost all the children living in the area attend the local comprehensive. There are also a small number of placing requests into the school. The distribution of male and female teachers in the school is very similar to that of Northwalls Academy.

Views of teaching as a career: positive features
There were commonalities between the men's and women's groups in relation to the aspects of teaching which they viewed as positive. These included an appreciation of the opportunity to see young people develop, doing a job which was 'really worthwhile' and 'giving something back' to society. Both men and women emphasised that teaching was 'not a job that bores you' and spoke of the benefits of a relatively autonomous working environment within the classroom. The following comment was typical of both the men's and women's groups:

> I would say that positive stuff about being a teacher is about giving something back and being involved in something that's really worthwhile. For somebody who is quite easily bored, it's not a job that bores you. (Female)

A woman teacher from a relatively disadvantaged background spoke of the opportunities for growth and development which teaching offered:

> I come from quite a working class background and you know, not to the same extent as some of the children in the school, but certainly one that was based on working class housing schemes initially, and I see the job as being quite prestigious, quite a step up. You know it's only in the last year or so that I can sort of believe that I am actually doing it.

The family-friendly hours provided by teaching were commented on by female teachers, but not by their male counterparts:

> . . . But the hours are definitely a benefit.
>
> I didn't find it a problem before I had the baby, but it's just trying to work with a child. I think as a working mother teaching is one of the

better career options when it comes to the hours in school, and when it comes to the holidays that match the children's – that's beneficial. So that's the plus points.

A number of male teachers had entered teaching after experiencing other working environments and commented positively on the greater satisfaction and autonomy within education compared with their previous employment which had quickly become predictable and mundane:

> Previous to this I worked in professional theatre and I just didn't feel that I was getting any satisfaction from my work helping others, and that was the big thought of getting into education so that I could say on a daily basis that the work that I was doing, the impact that it had on young people, was really worthwhile. So that's my big motivation.

> I worked in stockbrokers for five years before I came into teaching, so taking my experience from that into the classroom now, it's great. I see that it motivates pupils and it motivates me to see that. I get a lot of satisfaction from that to see someone learn from my own experience.

Views of teaching as a career: negative features

There was general agreement that teaching was an exhausting job and the pace of the working week was inherently stressful:

> The negative bit I think about teaching for me is the number of pupils that you see on a daily basis. We can end up seeing up to one hundred and eighty students on a daily basis and that is extremely stressful. You don't even notice you are getting stressed until you have a few days off. (Female)

The new demands of accountability and managerialism were seen to contribute to the pressure and detract from the enjoyment of teaching the subject:

> There are just numerous things, for example if you take the SQA returns, you have to keep assessment records for all year groups. As I say I don't know any other way round about it, referrals have to be handed in, punishment exercises have to be written, behaviour cards have to get filled in and this is all during your lesson or at the end of your lesson so that does take off time from your teaching . . . sometimes I feel as though I am chasing my tail, especially if I am teaching six periods a day. (Male)

First and second year science, you are rushing so much to get through each module and I mean I basically don't see the need to do that. That should be a time where you are enjoying it and you are building foundations . . . there should be time to actually sit back and enjoy it. (Female)

Men were rather more likely than women to complain about the relatively poor promotion prospects in teaching:

I also think men are probably looking at promotion, there's absolutely no promotion. At twenty-five you have got nowhere to go in the next forty years, got nowhere to go. There's no head of physics, there's no assistant head of guidance, there's no promotion, there's nothing anymore. (Male)

In the men's focus group in the rural secondary school, a perceived decline in pupil behaviour was seen as a problem. Discipline problems tended to be 'low level' but 'wearing', and teachers had to work hard to earn respect. Where children had little or no respect for their parents, the challenge to teachers was heightened. One teacher, however, felt that working with challenging young people was also a satisfying aspect of the job:

You know there is a smashing wee person inside but they haven't been taught that . . . so you sometimes feel you are a policeman, a social worker, a substitute parent . . .Yet our hands are tied behind our back with what we can say, what we can't say, what we can do, what we can't do. We know how accountable we are in this school.

The women's focus group also felt that the demands of inclusion made teaching more difficult:

There are more and more expectations on school and teachers to sort society out. We are the ones that can sort out bullying, drugs, everything. So whereas respect for us as a profession has gone down, both with children and with other adults, the responsibility that we are given has increased and that's difficult.

Interestingly, the teachers in the urban school with a diverse catchment area were much more positive about inclusion and working with challenging pupils than teachers in the rural school serving a more affluent neighbourhood.

There was inevitably some disagreement between teachers with regard to the positive and negative features of the job. For example, one teacher at Northwalls Academy commented on his dislike of development work, whereas another male teacher at the school said that the intellectual challenge of developing new programmes was one of the most satisfying aspects of his work.

It was felt that the declining public status of teaching was due to a number of factors, including a sustained campaign in the Thatcher era to denigrate teachers and an overwhelmingly negative press. Politicians and trades unions were also blamed for reinforcing negative stereotypes of teachers and teaching. A male teacher spoke of the need for teachers and their unions to draw attention to the positive aspects of education rather than always dwelling on the negative.

Reasons for the declining number of men in teaching

There was general agreement between the focus groups that the main reason for the declining number of men in teaching was the perception that the salary was not competitive with other professional jobs, particularly in the private sector:

> The comparative jobs in industry and other professions are going to pay a lot more than they do in teaching. There is no doubt about that. (Male)

Teachers were committed to the profession but one teacher commented:

> I can walk out the door and double my salary, or triple my salary . . . There is not a huge incentive to be here except to teach. (Male)

There was a suggestion that able people from minority ethnic groups might be encouraged to seek employment in other professions with much better remuneration. A female teacher described how her cousin was dissuaded from a career change into teaching because of its low status:

> I am thinking about one of my cousins who had a good job as a personnel manager, it was with [large retail firm]. Now when my cousin said he really hated his job so he didn't want to do that job any more and he was thinking of going into primary teaching, my mum was horrified. She says, 'No way, you can't do that, look at the job you have got, look at the good money you are earning and why do you want to be a primary teacher?' He didn't go into training or anything; he has now got another job. But for boys I think you know they look at their peers as well and you know they are maybe earning more money and they are thinking, as my cousin did . . . so I think a lot of the times it is a money issue for boys.

It was noted that many men still believed they had to be the main breadwinner to support their partner through periods of maternity leave and part-time work, and high house prices placed even more pressure on the main breadwinner.

There was also a belief that the nature of secondary school teaching had changed, so that increasingly teachers were expected to relate to children as individuals rather than simply teaching a subject. There was discussion in the women's focus group at Northwalls Academy as to whether women were inherently more suited to teaching than men:

> I think it's just that men look for different things in a career don't they, and it's possible that a lot of the traits that you need for teaching are predominantly female traits . . . I think caring, sensitivity, understanding, also wanting to put something back and to feel that you are doing something meaningful at your work, which I think is definitely less important for men. They probably want results, whereas women want to feel that they are doing something that really matters.

> But I would say as a rule generally it would appear that female teachers are much more likely to engage with kids and talk to them about something going on at home than male teachers who are much more likely, generally, it's a generalisation, not to do that in the same way.

Whereas primary school teaching has traditionally been perceived as drawing on women's ability to empathise with children, it appears that secondary school teaching may increasingly be understood in these terms and be regarded as less to do with imparting subject-based knowledge. However, whilst there was agreement that women might be more empathic than men, there was resistance to essentialist ideas of masculinity and femininity. One respondent said: 'It's not genetic, it's how they are raised.' Ultimately, having the right personal qualities rather than one's biological sex was regarded as the most important factor in determining who would be a good teacher:

> I think it's about the person, I really don't think it's anything to do with whether you are a man or whether you are a woman, I think it's about the person and I think if you have got certain qualities for teaching then you will be a good teacher . . . I think if the man has got the right attributes to be a teacher then it's totally appropriate that that's where he should be and very important for young boys that they do have role models . . . (Female)

A woman expressed the view that men were confused about their gender identity and were put off teaching because of its affective demands that might be seen as at variance with popular notions of masculinity.

The reduction in the number of men in teaching was seen as self-perpetuating, because 'the fewer men you have in teaching the less likely you are to attract men into a predominantly female teaching profession' (Female).

A counter example, however, was provided with regard to the increasing number of men in business and management departments in secondary schools, which in turn attracted more boys into the subject.

Whereas there was a cycle of decline in the number of men entering the profession, teaching continued to be attractive to women because of the formal acceptance of equal opportunities. A male teacher felt that women were attracted into teaching because it was one of the few occupations where they were guaranteed equal pay:

> I am just wondering if the gender balance with males and females is something to do with teaching being one of the few professions that women can compete equally with men, from a salary point of view. Because I think there is still in the twenty-first century this ridiculous situation where in certain professions some women are being paid less than men for doing the same job, and their route to promotion is sometimes blocked perhaps because of their gender. And I think women realise that if they come into education everybody is on an equal footing here, we are all going to earn the same money whether you get promoted or a normal teacher. And your route to promotion would be competing against men but this isn't going to be taken into consideration. As I say you kind of hope that in the industry it will disappear but I think it's still slightly ongoing.

Female teachers, on the other hand, felt that this rosy view of promotion opportunities was unrealistic and considered that the odds were still stacked in favour of men (see below).

Finally, women teachers felt that the growing awareness of child abuse and high profile cases reported in the media might act as a deterrent, particularly to men:

> The allegations that could be made is a really important thing too, but it's all about children's rights and if they wanted to make any allegations about any of us we are very vulnerable to that.

Views about primary teaching

Primary school teaching, it was believed, was not seen as sufficiently intellectually challenging by men:

> Because there's not the same academic challenge for men at primary levels as at secondary and you know in like nursery education, you never find a man there because it's not high powered enough for men. (Female)

A woman said that she felt that men would regard primary school teaching as simply 'baby sitting', and that the importance of child development was not sufficiently appreciated:

I mean traditionally you know men or people are seeing that as a woman's role to look after children at that age. I know it's all changing now and I think maybe men are changing as well. They will look after their own children fine but they are not going to look after other people's children as well, they may see it as babysitting basically when it comes to primary one and primary two.

As in secondary, it was felt that the lack of men in primary teaching had a cumulative effect, conveying the idea to the next generation of boys that primary teaching is not appropriate work for a man:

I think the lack of primary male teachers is a big issue as well because it's much higher female teachers isn't it in primary than it is in secondary. I think probably it's just a knock-on effect, young boys are seeing less and less role models as they go through school so they are possibly less likely to see it as something for them. (Female)

One man said that his mother had discouraged him from thinking about a career in primary teaching because the conversation in the staff room would be 'all babies and knitting'. Ironically, his decision to become a physics teacher in a secondary school meant that he was working with 'all old men':

My mum always said, 'You shouldn't be a primary teacher' and I said, 'Why not?' and she said 'All they talk about is babies and knitting because they are all women.' Now I can talk about babies and knitting no problem, babies are my thing, but I see the point, because I teach in physics and it's all men, and all old men . . .

Desirability of gender balance in teaching

There was agreement that achieving a reasonable balance between women and men in teaching was desirable for a range of reasons. Sometimes this reflected a negative attitude towards the dominance of women in certain parts of the education system. For example, a male teacher commented on the advantages of having more men in traditionally female areas, such as drama, which was traditionally 'all flowing clothes and pretending to be trees'. The benefit of having more men in business studies was also mentioned:

Business education has always been thought of as typing and that's all. But now you have got business management and I think the word management is attracting more men and it's attracting boys and I think that's fantastic to progress the subject socially and academically. Because it's a broad subject and everyone gets something from each part of the business education department. That's wonderful in my eyes and if it continues in that way and if more men come into the subject it will improve, or develop. (Male)

Home economics was identified as another subject area where the presence of a man appeared to have made the subject more appealing to boys:

> In standard grade we have managed to get half boys, half girls in our standard grade classes, which is quite interesting. It's not all due to the fact that we have got a male home economics teacher in the department just now, but some of it is due to that, just breaking down barriers. We haven't had parents asking us probably for about two years 'Oh, is that not a girls' thing?' They don't ask any more because they see what's happening in school and they have got cousins or older siblings. (Female)

The benefits of a good gender balance were likely to be felt by both teachers and pupils:

> If you have a department where you are all like-minded, you all go down the same line and no-one diverts from their line or level of thought, it can become very regimented, strict, and there's no variety there, there is nothing to stimulate the pupils. I just feel there should be different areas that the teachers within the department specialise in and also use their personality to improve the area that they have chosen to specialise in. (Male)

Promotion opportunities

Women in the secondary school focus groups believed that their male counterparts were more strategic in their approach to their career and were more likely to be promoted as a result of sponsorship by more senior men:

> I think in some ways they are being coached in a way and maybe that's unfair, but I think that things that they do are noticed more than the things we do . . . I mean you are doing clubs at lunchtime, has anybody ever come up to you and said 'Do you fancy a wee bit of promotion here, fancy doing this?' You know maybe it's our fault, maybe we don't highlight the things we are doing and the males do . . .

> I don't think women put themselves forward and I have ruled out ever being a principal teacher because I just wouldn't want to have that job. I have ruled that out so I don't want promotion, whereas young men put themselves forward . . . But the second thing is that if there's males at the top of the school, obviously they are looking for people to do the job as well as they did and that will be replicated in themselves won't it, so young men will be much more suitable than young women, and young black women in particular.

Women believed that they were motivated by an intrinsic love of the job rather than a desire for advancement:

> You are doing these clubs because of the enjoyment, you are not doing it for your CV, whereas it might be unfair but you definitely get the impression that the young dynamic male members of staff might be sort of building a profile up towards promotion.

Whilst their female counterparts believed that the promotion odds were stacked in favour of men, male teachers were very gloomy about their promotion chances and this was a key factor in diminishing their enthusiasm for the job (see above). However, it was evident that promotion aspirations had not been abandoned. A man in his late twenties said that he was already applying for Head of Faculty jobs not because he expected to get them, but to get the interview experience. He was able to comment in detail about the relative pay differential between the bottom of the deputy head scale and the top of the head of faculty scale.

Positive actions to attract more men into teaching

As we noted at the start of this book, during the first half of the twentieth century radical action in favour of male teachers was implemented in the form of a bar on the employment of women teachers after marriage. Subsequently, enhanced pay for male teachers was seen as an appropriate means of halting the 'feminisation' of teaching. None of our respondents proposed such radical actions in favour of men. Rather, a number of suggestions were made with regard to making teaching more appealing to both women and men.

It was felt that careers talks at school should emphasise the positive features of teaching as a career for men:

> Maybe the career talks and what not at schools should let the kids be aware of the possibilities of promotion, how they could climb the career ladder or where it could get them, be very realistic about that and let them see you don't have to be just in the classroom. If you want to be that's fine, but if you don't want to be in the classroom you can get into management. (Female)

Efforts should be made to attract men into primary teaching at a later point in their lives when they were more mature:

> I think most eighteen-year-old boys would just think it was a bit naff to be a primary teacher at that age. I don't think they would be mature enough to deal with the idea. (Female)

Male focus group members felt better pay would attract more men into teaching and teacher training should be staffed by people who had more recent classroom experience. In addition, there was a need for more male teachers who could be 'shining examples' as role models. The pleasure of working with young people should also be emphasised.

Primary school focus groups

In this section, we summarise findings from the primary school focus groups. Participants were drawn from different year groups and the majority were women, although there were two male respondents in each group. Most respondents were non-promoted teachers.

Westside Primary: school background

The school is a medium sized primary with 220 primary places and an additional 60 nursery places. In addition to the teaching staff there are a number of learning assistants, nursery nurses and a full time education home visitor. The school was opened in August 2003 and is very well equipped with attractive grounds and Astro-turf pitches. It serves an area of multiple deprivation on the edge of the city.

Hilltop Primary: school background

This is a large primary school in a rural local authority area. The community it serves contains pockets of deprivation, but is relatively affluent in the national context.

Views of teaching as a career: positive features

All the staff talked about the job satisfaction that comes from working with children, suggesting that the main qualification for entering teaching was that 'you really have to like kids' (Female), otherwise the job would not be enjoyable. One female respondent suggested:

> I think working in direct contact with the children is good fun and you are constantly learning something new everyday. You learn a lot about yourself and you learn a lot about them.

There was also the camaraderie that came from engaging in out-of work activities with people who were also teachers. This seemed to be particularly important for the male teachers, with one teacher describing the primary school teachers' football team that operated in one of the cities. He suggested:

> There is a male primary staff football team and a lot of my friends are still playing. That is the sort of male thing. I think that is quite important as it brings young teachers in. You go into the changing room and you have all got something in common. It also takes it out of your own classroom so you get a wider view.

This appears to be an example of a typically male activity being used to reinforce masculine gender identity, which might be challenged by working in a predominantly female environment. Another positive feature was the variety of the job. One suggested:

> People get stuck in a rut [in other posts] but here two days are never the same. The problems that crop up are different every day and I think that is a really strong benefit. (Female)

The benefits were summarised by one respondent as 'You are not bored. You can have a laugh. It is quite good fun' (Male). All agreed that the long holidays 'were a big perk', especially for those that had childcare responsibilities. A final positive feature was the variety of people that they met 'so many different people outside the school' (Female). This 'pastoral care aspect' that involved interacting with a variety of people was seen as 'both interesting and fun' (Male).

Views of teaching as a career: negative features

The key negative aspect was the exhausting demands of the job both emotionally and in terms of time commitments:

> There aren't enough hours in the day to think, over and above the actual contact with the children. It is quite hard. (Female)

The respondents pointed out that 'there is always quite a lot to take on board over and above what you do during the day' (Female) because of the need to keep up with changing policies such as healthy eating. One of the male teachers who had been teaching for twenty-five years pointed out:

> There are so many new priorities that you sometimes feel you are skimming the surface . . . and never really doing anything properly.

He also pointed out that 'it is really hard for a teacher to refresh themselves. There is no going somewhere else where you can take time out, I think it is really difficult'. Teachers, it was suggested, were also seen by politicians as being responsible for solving all kinds of problems. As another male teacher explained:

> I don't want to be negative but it doesn't matter what it is, we have to change it because that is what society wants us to do. Everything is down to us.

Reasons for gender imbalance in teaching

A key reason given for men not to enter teaching was the poor salary. One male respondent suggested:

teachers are really poorly paid in comparison to the wider world. If you have one wage ... it is really difficult. Many teachers who have got a family tend to have their wife working as well. It is not an attractive salary. The way society sees us you are expected to be the breadwinner.

Another male teacher recounted how his father had tried to dissuade him from primary teaching because:

My mum worked as a primary teacher when she was younger and my father saw it as women's work. But I have always enjoyed working with children and I had a lot of work babysitting and looking after and playing with cousins and things like this. I had actually always really enjoyed that part of my life. I was very comfortable around children and I just took it from there.

He enjoyed the hands-on work but it was thought that some males might feel a bit more daunted by the 'more nurturing type of education that occurs in nursery and primary 1'. This also raised other questions such as, 'Is it socially acceptable for this child to sit on my knee in assembly? (Male). This led to men needing to be 'more aware of keeping yourself safe' (Male).

There was also the perceived low status of teaching that made it less attractive to men. 'I think males are also drawn to the status thing. It is not as high as being a doctor or a lawyer so it is less attractive' (Female). The dominance of females in the profession also lowered the status: 'I don't know how you would get round the barrier of men seeing it as a female dominated profession' (Male).

One of the female teachers pointed out that although it was family-friendly in theory, 'it is extraordinarily hard work so it does not necessarily benefit those with child-care responsibilities'. A final problem was the 'bad press about the discipline issues in education maybe puts people off. Not just men, women too, but the fact that men are usually pushed towards the harder classes' acts as an additional deterrent (Female). It was suggested that women might be better at dealing with discipline problems than men and therefore be less deterred by the perceived decline in pupil behaviour:

I have two boys and I have suggested teaching to them at various points over the years, but it is the hassle they would get . . . they couldn't put up with the cheek they would have to take . . . If they were teaching they wouldn't like the bad behaviour . . . they would find that difficult to deal with...and I think women can maybe take it more. (Female)

Desirability of gender balance in teaching

The group all felt that there should be more men in primary teaching. One pointed out:

> In a society where so many children don't have a male role model, at home or within their immediate sphere of communication, a male teacher can actually be really important. (Female)

However, another suggested:

> I think it is also difficult as well as there is a contradiction because men are quite often pushed towards the difficult class therefore they have to fulfil that stereotype of being able to deal with the difficult class. What quite often children need are men that are quiet, softly spoken and gentle. That is actually really important. (Male)

Respondents also suggested that men brought different approaches and interests to teaching. One male teacher said 'I really like and know about football and [so I can] talk about it at the same level as they do'. One of the females suggested that 'You [men] can probably do other things [such as] tease the girls in a way that a woman teacher wouldn't. [Men] can [have] a different relationship with pupils.' This different approach included being:

> more over the top, more dramatic, more fun loving. Females tend to be more controlled whereas the male teachers put a more humorous slant on it which boys and girls like. (Female)

Promotion opportunities

Respondents all agreed that men in primary education were expected to seek promotion even if they might not want to. One male teacher said:

> There is a huge expectation for males to be promoted. And I don't think that is necessarily a good thing because a lot of people are great class teachers. [They are] very happy in the classroom and they are not born administrators, they are not born managers, but males are perceived that that is the role for them. I can't think of many males of my age group, my peers, who haven't gone up the ladder beyond the classroom. So it is very unusual to find somebody [like me] who won't do that.

Another male teacher said: 'I have worked with female teachers who have said to me "When are you going to go for your depute headship?" and I turn around and say "I don't want to do that." One of the female teachers agreed that primary head teachers really pushed male teachers. A male teacher that she trained with found that his head teacher was 'really concentrating on what was good for his promotion prospects and he is not particularly interested in being out of the classroom but he was getting a lot of pressure from her'.

Our respondents also reflected on the disadvantages of being a head teacher. One male teacher suggested:

> Although there is some administrative work as a teacher, there is a completely different level when you are a head teacher and increasingly so. You do become removed from the teachers. Head teachers are managers. They do not teach anymore. [It's also more difficult] because they are not taught how to manage. They are expected to learn on the job.

On the other hand, women were seen as enjoying the classroom experience and the direct contact with children. One male suggested 'my wife is a teacher too and she is not interested at all in promotion. She would just shrivel up if she got promoted out of class. She loves her day-to-day contact.' It appears that, in these respondents' experience, women and men are treated quite differently in relation to promotion opportunities in the primary sector.

Positive actions to attract more men into teaching

Respondents had a few suggestions that might attract more men into the profession but whatever action was taken 'the baseline is you have got to like children' (Female). Teaching was seen as vocational, so 'If you are only interested in money, don't go into teaching [because] it is not worth it' (Male). Another agreed, 'Being the breadwinner, once you are in the system you have got the mortgage, it is really hard to downsize your income especially when you start on a probationer's salary' (Female).

On the other hand it was suggested that men might possibly consider teaching as a second career option, especially if they had experience of redundancy in their current occupation. One of the female teachers suggested that teaching might be attractive to 'somebody who came from that background into a permanent teaching post that was secure'. Changing careers was seen as positive for the profession because 'I think the experiences that people from other careers bring into the job are really valid and important'. Another added:

> I think a lot of guys go out and earn their big bucks and become a bit disillusioned with that. They've maybe even made a bit of money and they see that that isn't everything. Yet they then have the maturity, different experiences and skills, maybe become fathers and think 'that might be something for me'.

Another suggestion was that a lot of other people's jobs are tedious whereas 'in teaching there is always something going on', so this should be promoted in any advertising campaigns. It was also suggested that this might appeal more to men because they were more interested in variety and more likely to have demanding but boring jobs. Part of this was the job satisfaction that comes from 'seeing that progress is being made, which is very rewarding' (Male). Teaching was seen as being able to offer both security and variety where 'every day is different' (Male) and this should appeal to those that liked working with people.

Finally the long holidays were seen as attractive. 'I think a lot of my friends who are not teachers and who are male, are envious of the holidays' (Male). A female teacher felt that advertising campaigns should emphasise the long holidays and relatively generous pension as part of the overall remuneration package:

> The long holidays, which is the big perk, are built into the salary. You know sometimes you see the adverts now, a job advertised 'plus pension' which makes up your total remuneration. We have got long holidays as part of our remuneration.

Summary and conclusion

Staff working in both the secondary and primary sectors agreed that there were a number of positive aspects of teaching. These included opportunities to contribute to the social and academic development of children and young people and the variety and autonomy it gave them. They found that the holidays and pension were positive features compared with jobs in the private sector and that the working hours are very good for people with childcare responsibilities. A few respondents noted, however, that the sheer hard work of teaching made it difficult for those with family responsibilities despite the benefit of the holidays.

There were some negative features, particularly in secondary schools, which included the stress of large numbers of pupils and time-consuming paperwork that took time away from teaching. A number of respondents suggested that the media and politicians sometimes promoted negative views of teachers' professional competence. Lack of promotion and low pay in comparison with some other professions such as medicine and the law was highlighted by male teachers but not by females.

The following two points were made forcefully in some of the focus groups, but not by teachers in the urban secondary school, the school serving the most diverse community. They argued that society has unrealistic expectations of what teachers can achieve in terms of dealing with a range of social ills. In addition, discipline problems, highlighted by the media and trades unions, make teaching a less attractive career choice.

In giving reasons for the declining number of men in teaching, many respondents identified factors that were about gendered identities and their consequences. Many suggested that the perception of teaching as a woman's job, particularly in the primary sector, made it less attractive to men. In addition a focus on child protection issues may make men feel vulnerable, particularly those working with young children. Another factor was that many men regarded themselves as the principal family breadwinner and believed that they would be better paid in industry and other professions even though, as we have indicated in Chapter 3, these may be unrealistic expectations. In addition, it was noted that there had been changes in the conceptualisation of teaching particularly at secondary level, where empathy with children and young people was seen as just as important as subject knowledge. Women might find it easier than men to respond to the emotional demands of the job. Primary teaching might lack intellectual challenge for men and be seen as 'baby-sitting', or alternatively men might be constructed as the disciplinarians and be given the difficult classes.

These gendered stereotypes were both reported and challenged by our respondents who felt that they did not personally hold such views but were reporting on those that predominated in society. In many ways the male primary teachers we interviewed showed how they had to confront these gender stereotypes on a daily basis but took individual routes. For some their masculine identity was asserted through the pursuit of traditionally male pursuits in their leisure time as in the primary men's football team. For others, who were more comfortable with their identity and had a more altru-istic orientation, these traditional pursuits were of less interest.

Gendered identities also impacted on promotion opportunities with the assumption that 'women teach and men manage' (Acker, 1994) still quite dominant. Our women respondents felt that men are likely to be given much greater informal sponsorship and mentoring which enhanced their promo-tion opportunities and were more strategic in their career management strat-egies. On the other hand some men in the primary sector felt pressurised into seeking promotion when they would rather stay in the classroom. Whilst the formalisation of equal opportunities made the job more attractive to women, it had led some men to feel they had more competition for promotion. This was particularly apparent in the secondary sector where some men felt they had poorer promotion opportunities following the recent flattening of the career structure and this had had a negative effect on their morale.

The managerialist regimes in schools were criticised due to the excessive bureaucracy that they generated and increased regulation and accountability requirements. However, there was no association of this regime with either masculinity or femininity on the part of our respondents. Neither did the staff identify particular differences between male and female head teachers in their management styles or ability to cope with the demands of accountability.

Many respondents pointed out the lack of male teachers especially in the early stages of primary and felt that boys, particularly those in single parent families, benefited from positive role models. Interestingly, teachers did not argue the case that more men in teaching would solve the problems of boys' under-achievement. Rather, it was suggested that men bring diverse interests and personality traits into teaching and so are particularly welcome in previously female-dominated areas such as business and home economics. Most respondents sought a gender-balanced team as this affected a range of factors such as the atmosphere in the staffroom, the broadening of the range of interests offered and different styles of teaching.

Positive messages about teaching need to be promoted through advertising campaigns and other means such as emphasising improved pay; good pensions and holidays; opportunities for working with young people and doing really worthwhile work. Negative messages about teachers and teaching, sometimes transmitted by the media, trades unions and politicians, should be downplayed, with more attention paid to positive aspects of the job. Careers work at schools and universities could be targeted more closely on boys and young men. The advantages of teaching for those wishing a mid-life change in career should also be highlighted.

As discussed in Chapter 4, two distinct discourses were associated with the issue of identifying and redressing the growing gender imbalance in teaching. According to some teachers, attracting more men into teaching was crucial in providing positive role models, whilst others maintained that biological sex was irrelevant, whilst dedication to the job and the ability to empathise with a wide range of pupils was critical. Implicitly, these views reflect different positions with regard to the embodiment of gender, which are discussed further in Chapter 6.

Chapter 6

CONCLUSION

Lyn Tett and Sheila Riddell

Introduction
In this chapter we return to the central themes of the book set out in Chapter 1 in order to address some key questions about the causes of the declining proportion of men in teaching despite their continued domination of promoted positions, the consequences of the shifting gender balance and the action that might be taken to address the current situation.

Gender identity and employment
In order to explore why only a declining proportion of men choose teaching, we need to look at how earlier choices are made. It is evident that subject choices at secondary school are highly gendered (Croxford, 2000; Gaskell, 1992), with girls and boys continuing to adhere to stereotypical notions of 'male' and 'female' occupations despite the broadening of the curriculum and wider possibilities for occupational choice. This phenomenon can in part be explained by the theory of stereotyping wherein 'stereotypes' link a social category with particular attributes (e.g. women are caring and emotional). Such stereotypes are extended to perceptions of ability, and in the case of occupational stereotypes, abilities at different jobs. Gender is constructed as relational, and as a foundational aspect of identity. Pupils may draw on 'gender appropriate' curriculum subjects and occupational choices to bolster their constructions of gender identity. Moreover, pupils draw on what they know to inform these constructions and tend to make choices they deem appropriate for people like them and these are gendered, classed and raced (Osgood *et al.*, 2006, p. 312).

Francis *et al.* (2003) argue that the reason there is little overlap between the jobs chosen by girls and boys, despite increased opportunity, is that the attributes of the jobs they choose are stereotypically gendered. Girls tend to choose jobs with attributes that can be classed as 'caring' or 'creative', while boys choose jobs with scientific, technical or business oriented features.

The subjects that are studied post-16 are also highly gendered, with girls more often opting for subjects in the areas of arts and humanities which have cultural value, whilst boys more frequently choose science and technical subjects which may have greater exchange value in the labour market (Osgood *et al.*, 2006, p. 310). Even girls studying science and technology are more likely to use their qualifications to teach, rather than to enter an occupation where men predominate.

Unlike women, men working in non-traditional occupations have been found to benefit from their token status through the assumption of enhanced leadership and other skills and by being associated with a more careerist attitude to work (Simpson, 2004). Men are more likely to monopolise positions of power and to be rewarded for their difference from women in terms of higher pay and other benefits. Unlike women in non-traditional careers, men appear to gain from their high visibility and assumptions about their authority, as it exposes them to situations that demand initiative and resourcefulness.

Our data show that in primary teaching men recognised that their minority status gave them career advantages, for example, selection boards were perceived to look favourably on male applicants on the grounds that they would provide a role model for the male pupils. In addition assumptions of male careerism meant that men were given opportunities to acquire skills and expertise, for example, by going on courses that would improve their chances of promotion. In addition, men experienced differential treatment, for example, female administrative staff were more likely to be accommodating to requests for photocopying, printing and typing and younger men tended to be 'mothered' by older female colleagues. Many respondents spoke of the way men were encouraged to seek promotion, as it was assumed that they were more interested in a career than their female colleagues. None of the men we interviewed felt isolated or marginalised at work, despite their minority status. Their relations with women were perceived as positive and a source of comfort and they commented on how much they liked women and how they enjoyed their company.

All these factors make it more likely that men will be promoted, but some men felt that they were pushed into management as a more acceptable masculine role. Sometimes this was because of suspicion from parents and others who regarded men, particularly those involved with young children, as suspect. As we saw in Chapter 4, issues around the protection of children became conflated with ideas about masculinity, leading to mistrust of men as classroom teachers. These anxieties were also reflected in the male teachers' concerns about their interactions with children reported in Chapter 5. Being pushed into management roles was particularly unwelcome for men who were in their second career and looking for a more interactive role with children.

Men in secondary teaching were more fretful about their promotion chances than those in primary and complained about the post-McCrone faculty structure (see Chapter 5). Some male teachers recognised that their status as men gave them greater authority than their female counterparts. For example, they felt that they commanded greater respect from older pupils, which meant that they experienced fewer discipline problems than some female staff. We also saw that women perceive men as being more careerist, strategic and heavily sponsored by senior men although men often seemed unaware of the gendered benefits they were receiving. Their female colleagues and other key informants also showed that there were still sexist attitudes on the part of school board members and councillors about men being more suitable for headships in large secondary schools.

A final issue relates to work orientations and the economy in Scotland where there are other, more interesting and lucrative options available in science, engineering and information technology, where men still dominate. Despite complaints about the intensity of work in teaching, it is still generally seen as a family-friendly job, with long holidays coinciding with children's holidays. Even undergraduates who were negative about the profession recognised this as a positive feature. Although some teachers pointed out that it is very demanding of time, and thus not particularly family- friendly, compared with any equivalent profession it is highly compatible with raising a family. Since women are more likely than men to be clustered in the adaptive/family centred groups in terms of work orientation (Hakim, 2004; Crompton, 2006), the possibility of combining a career in teaching with having a family seems to appeal to them particularly strongly. A sign of serious changes in men's approach to work and family life might well be signalled by a greater appreciation of this aspect of teaching.

With regard to women's and men's own accounts of the factors influencing their work orientation, it was evident that women in particular recognised the influence of both personal choices and social structures on their lives and work-related decisions. Women teachers in secondary schools recognised that they still bore the main responsibility for childcare, which attracted them to teaching as a potentially compatible occupation. They also felt that men were influenced against teaching by relatives and friends because of the expectation that they would be the main breadwinner for the larger part of their working lives. However, women did not believe that this socially constructed sexual division of labour justified overt or covert discrimination against them in the workplace. There were complaints, for example, that the Chartered Teacher Programme was less accessible to part-time workers most of whom were women, and the greater sponsorship of male teachers was also seen as unfair. Men, by way of contrast, were clearly more career orientated, but were less reflective of the social pressures which made this the case. In general, it would appear that the ongoing debate in the field of gender and employment is too polarised. Whilst one camp maintains that gender divisions in the labour market are a product of personal choice (Hakim, 2004), and another emphasises social structures (Crompton, 2006), evidence from this research suggests that there may be an interplay of these two elements, reflected in people's accounts of their own experiences.

The decline of men in teaching and the 'problem of boys'

As discussed earlier, there is widespread concern throughout the English-speaking world with regard to the growing 'feminisation' of teaching and its assumed detrimental effects on boys. Those arguing for radical action to increase the proportion of men in teaching maintain that boys' social constructions of masculinity are fragile, rest on group affirmation and are therefore easily undermined. It is maintained that any damage to masculine identity is likely to have powerful consequences for boys' personal self-esteem and social positioning (Mac an Ghaill, 1996; Skelton, 2003; Tinklin *et al.*, 2005). Children and young people of school age are at a crucial stage of development, as they seek to construct 'acceptable' versions of masculinity. In the absence of positive male role models in school, it is argued that boys, particularly those from socially disadvantaged backgrounds, are likely to reject education on the grounds that academic endeavour is an effete activity favoured by girls and women. Those they seek to emulate may have failed within the education system and operate on the margins of the labour market.

Critics of this approach (Mills *et al.*, 2004; Roulston and Mills, 2000) suggest that much depends on the style of masculinity adopted by male teachers in school and their own ability to model progressive versions of masculinity. The literature suggests that, whilst work is often central to male identity (Francis, 2002; Franks, 1999; Miller *et al.*, 2004), particular challenges may arise for those choosing to work in non-traditional areas. According to Kimmel (1994) and Connell (1996), men scrutinise each other for signs of femininity and men in conventionally female roles fear the disapproval of other men so they need to take steps to reassert their masculinity. A study by Simpson (2004) found that atypical men manage this by reconstructing their job so as to minimise its non-masculine associations. For example, in primary school teaching the men in Simpson's study re-cast the job content to emphasise the 'male' components such as highlighting the importance of sport or the benefits of providing a role model for male pupils. Another strategy was to create meaning around the job in ways that highlighted 'masculine' characteristics. Such characteristics were often associated with special skill requirements that were seen as essentially male (e.g. coping under stress) and the nature of the job that was seen to embody 'masculine' qualities (e.g. excitement, challenge).

The data reported in Chapter 5 show that these compensatory gendered practices did indeed take place on the part of the male primary teachers, for example, sport was highlighted by one of the male primary teachers not only as something he was interested in and could contribute to the school, but also as a way of relating to other men in primary teaching through the city-wide football team. Female respondents noted that men might see primary teaching in particular as an unsuitable occupation because it was 'not a proper job for a man' and was 'not sufficiently intellectually challenging'. At the same time, they noted that men in teaching adopted modes of behaviour to deliberately distinguish themselves from women. They were 'more over the top' and offered more excitement and challenge to pupils than female teachers could. Whilst almost all the respondents, regardless of gender, emphasised the importance of having male role models to highlight positive masculine characteristics, it is evident that the type of masculinity modelled is critical. Devotion to sport, for example, can be used to corral boys and men into a particular version of masculinity which may be underpinned by the threat of violence (Mac an Ghaill, 1994).

It was evident from the accounts of some of our respondents that some men in teaching are likely to exemplify non-typical masculine characteristics. For example, those who have moved from a traditionally masculine field may want to remain close to professional practice and be reluctant to take on managerial and leadership positions as we saw in Chapter 5. Their approach to their new occupation appears to reflect disillusionment with the rewards of the male 'careerist' model of steady progression and increases in status and power. Several of our key informants in Chapter 4 suggested that the men who had become disillusioned with their previous highly demanding and often insecure jobs had a great deal to offer teaching and might provide alternative models of masculinity for boys to emulate.

It is also evident from the literature on the career choices of graduates that the use of career choice in identity formation, in relation to teaching and other 'caring' professions, is not straightforward (Thornton and Bricheno, 2003; Whitehead, 2002). Some masculine identities are formed in varying degrees of opposition to overarching patterns so, for example, the male student teachers who participated in Drudy *et al.*'s study (2005, p. 36) showed considerably greater orientation to caring than other male school leavers. This would suggest that men who do choose teaching, especially in the primary sector, differ from the general male population with regard to a number of characteristics. Johnson *et al.* (1999, p. 61) also found that men who had chosen primary teaching as a career saw it as a job in which their 'maleness was necessary and of value', whilst at the same time recognising that teaching 'was suited to women but not exclusively a woman's job'.

Gender, new managerialism and inclusion

As noted in Chapter 1, there have been major changes over recent years in the climate of Scottish schools, with the growth of regulation and accountability regimes on the one hand and, on the other, an emphasis on inclusion and the need to build supportive and empathic relationships with pupils. Feminists writing about the growth of new managerialism in various spheres of education (Davies, 2003; Deem, 1998, Mahony, 2000; Ozga and Walker, 1999) were gloomy about the impact of its 'surveillance and control' mechanisms, which, it was believed, would inevitably dampen creativity and prove particularly damaging to women because of the masculinist styles of work and management likely to be fostered. However, in our study the intensification of work associated with new managerialism was actually seen in more negative terms by men than women, with male respondents more likely to complain about increased paperwork, whilst women said that they were more organised and thus better able to respond to the increased demand for planning and record keeping. It is also noticeable that the proportion of women participating in the Scottish Qualification for Headship has greatly increased over recent years, suggesting that, far from being deterred from considering a move into management, women are more likely to consider moving into a management position. It is also the case that equality policies are being increasingly implemented through managerialist strategies. For example, the public sector duty on gender, implemented from 2007, will require institutions to plan to increase the proportion of women in management and to monitor change over time. This raises the important question of whether equality goals can be pursued effectively through managerialist strategies (Riddell *et al.*, 2007).

There was also evidence from the research to support the idea that the emphasis on inclusion and relationship-building in school might be less readily accepted by men than women. Teachers of both sexes in some, but not all, schools complained about the growing social expectation that they would be able to compensate for a wide range of social problems. The responses to the undergraduate survey and the key informants suggested that men were more interested in using their subject knowledge than women and were less interested in people-orientated work. Those considering a career in teaching, the majority of whom were women, were significantly less likely to agree with the statement that discipline problems made teaching an unattractive option. Women in one of the secondary school focus groups argued strongly that men were more interested in promotion than 'going the extra mile' with an individual pupil. Overall, there was considerable evidence to support the view that the greater focus on negotiation with pupils and inclusion of pupils at the margins, with possibly less focus on communicating subject knowledge in secondary schools, might be more appealing to women than men.

What are the consequences of the shifting gender balance in teaching and does it matter?

There are competing views with regard to whether the growing gender imbalance in teaching is a particular problem or not. As we noted in Chapters 4 and 5, the majority of our respondents believed that the sex of teachers was a salient factor, and the ideal was to have an even balance of men and women so that boys and girls could observe the enactment of a range of versions of masculinity and femininity. At the same time, there was a counter-narrative which suggested that the sex of teachers was irrelevant, and what really mattered was the quality of the teacher's professional practice and the presence of varied gender identities, which could be embodied by either men or women. This, of course, encapsulates one of the major debates within recent feminist thinking. On the one hand, bodies such as the Equal Opportunities Commission and, in future, the Commission for Equality and Human Rights, are based on the assumption that a person's biological sex is important, since inequality is structured around such difference. Arguments made by political theorists such as Phillips (2004) maintain that the goal should be to pursue equality of outcome for men and women. Butler (1990), on the other hand, would argue for a blurring of the distinction between sex and gender, suggesting that the assumption of a binary divide based on sex is misplaced. The focus instead should be on the exploration of how gender is performed, which might or might not map onto biological sex. According to this line of thinking, attempts to count the number of women and men in particular occupational groups, and to remedy disproportionalities, is fundamentally misguided. There is thus a yawning gap between applied equality policies, sometimes referred to as 'strategic essentialism', and post-structuralist theories of sex and gender.

Beyond the theoretical, there are also different views with regard to the practical consequences of the gender imbalance in teaching. On the positive side, having more women in the profession may lead to better interpersonal relationships between staff and pupils. The changing nature of secondary teaching, with a strong emphasis on inclusion as well as attainment, requires more altruistic and empathic orientations towards work and these are traditionally associated with women. Secondary schools dominated by women might be able to emulate the success of primary schools with a better ethos, fewer exclusions, more engaged pupils and a more caring atmosphere. Another advantage is that women may be more balanced and less competitive people, partly because of the work–life balance they seek and also because they do not invest everything in the job. They are thus able to exemplify a more humane and holistic approach to work, family and social life which might beneficially be adopted by both boys and girls. A final positive aspect of the growing proportion of women in teaching is that if traditionally masculine subjects such as physics and computing science are largely taught by women, then this will provide positive messages for girls about the suitability of the subject without necessarily deterring boys.

On the downside, the gender imbalance in teaching continues to propagate messages about outdated gender roles to the next generation of young people, since it is in schools that gender stereotypes may be confirmed or challenged. Another negative is that recruitment drives aimed overtly at men might reinforce established stereotypes of masculinity, and therefore could be detrimental to achieving gender equality in education. They may also reinforce an approach to boys' problem behaviour that views female teachers as less capable of teaching boys, whereas the real issue to be addressed is the way in which gendered relations of power are enacted between boys and female teachers (Mills *et al.*, 2004). Similarly, advertising specifically to attract men, for example, by drawing attention to the fact that men still occupy the highest paid jobs in teaching, might reinforce negative gender stereotypes from the outset, attract competitive careerist men, and possibly lead to the denigration of female teachers (Carrington and Skelton, 2003).

Attracting more men into teaching: what is to be done?

We can conclude from this that encouraging more men into teaching involves three kinds of actions. Firstly, it is important to discuss and challenge subject and work-experience choices early in a pupil's career so that it is possible for both boys and girls to make gender atypical choices with the minimum of barriers. Osgood *et al.* (2006) argue that neo-liberal, individualistic 'freedom of choice' approaches to equal opportunities have resulted in persistent gendered attitudes and experiences of work. If this is to change then schools must:

> Challenge structural inequalities and barriers in order to achieve greater diversity and non-traditional career pathways, pupils should be encouraged, directed and supported to experience a diversity of work experiences including those that are non-traditional (p. 318)

Another strategy when recruiting may be to emphasise the male aspects of the job by emphasising the challenge and excitement, the potential for developing interests in sport and the opportunities to provide a positive masculine role model. However, there are clearly problems in downplaying the caring and emotional aspects of the job that are seen as traditionally female, since these may implicitly denigrate women.

A final approach is to emphasise the pay and career opportunities now available in the profession. We have seen that men were more likely to complain about low pay in teaching. This may be because they expect to be the main family breadwinner, and certainly a number of respondents suggested that this was the case, whereas women may expect their wage to be constituent part of family income. However, despite the conviction amongst some men that they could walk out of the door into a more lucrative occupation, it is not clear that in reality other available jobs would pay more. Perhaps there is a time lag between the perception of low pay and the reality of the actual pay now available.

Many of our respondents thought that change was likely in the future and that the current position was simply historical. They suggested that the growth of female candidates for the qualification for headship and the increasing numbers of women at depute and principal level all indicated that promoted posts would become more evenly distributed within the next ten years. If these predictions are accurate then teaching would buck the trend in all other professions where men proportionally outnumber women.

In conclusion

Evidence from practising teachers suggests that whilst they make gendered occupational choices for themselves, most teachers also believe strongly that there should be no discriminatory barriers for others. Horizons and the zones of occupational possibilities that individuals are prepared to consider as suitable or appropriate are often limited to a range of quite highly gendered options. Adopting a 'gender autonomy' approach can expand the zone of possibilities people are prepared to consider for themselves. Gender autonomy is measured by 'the extent to which people can choose to follow typical or atypical paths without penalty or disadvantage' (Evans, 2004, p. 89). This applies to both material (dis)advantage and social (dis)approval. This means that a high level of occupational gender segregation is not necessarily negative as long as practices and policies are in place to enable both men and women to exercise gendered preferences without penalties or unfair advantages. For example in Nordic countries although women experience above the European average segregation in the labour market 'any disadvantages accruing to such work are more mitigated than elsewhere by the protection afforded by the high unionization of part-time work and the public sector as well as through generous social benefits' (Singh, 1998, p. 150). One aspect of the move to greater gender autonomy is to have fewer penalties and barriers for those who make atypical choices. This needs to be addressed both for atypical men in primary education and, just as importantly, for atypical women in promoted posts in both secondary and primary schools. Gender has to be built into pedagogical processes through greater attention to identity issues and the creation of supportive networks.

In the meantime, given the negative views of occupations which are predominantly female, it is important to continue to monitor the gender balance in teaching. As we have argued, schools and educational institutions in general are places where gender identities are constantly being negotiated, tested and enacted. This is why we need to take very seriously findings from the analysis of the statistical data which demonstrate the decline in men's participation in the teaching workforce in Scotland, and the findings from the undergraduate survey which show that there is little enthusiasm for teaching as a career amongst the next generation of potential teachers. As Anne Phillips points out, the aspirations that shape our choice are themselves framed by our social location, and the choices we make are constrained by the resources available to us and also by the ways in which preferences are formed (Phillips, 2004, p. 16). She suggests that where comparison between groups is concerned it makes sense to start from the expectation that all groups would normally be distributed in roughly equal proportions along all measures of social activity. This means that we should expect equality of outcome and take any divergence from this as a reasonably safe indication that opportunities are not equal (Phillips, 2004, p. 18).

Key informants and teachers generally appeared to support the broad case for equality of outcomes, not just opportunities, made by Phillips. They saw benefits in maintaining the diversity of the teaching profession, since all pupils could benefit from the range of interests and attributes offered by women and men. Men were particularly welcome in non-traditional areas such as Home Economics and Business Studies in secondary schools, since their example inspired pupils to think about non-traditional career choices. The belief that schools should reflect social diversity is also high up the political agenda as reflected in the review of initial teacher education recently conducted by the Scottish Executive (2005b).

The broad consensus from our informants was that whilst men should be encouraged into teaching through positive advertising campaigns, this should not be at the expense of women. The long-term answer probably lies in shifting men's and women's work orientations, so that they are more evenly distributed across the spectrum of work orientation. In the shorter term, given women's greater commitment to equality, it would be ironic if the new gender public sector duty to provide an equal gender balance in all sectors were to be used to promote men's interests in teaching above those of women.

REFERENCES

Acker, S. (1983) 'Women and teaching: a semi-detached sociology of a semi-profession', in Walker, S. and Barton, L. (eds) (1983) *Gender, Class and Education*, Lewes: Falmer Press, pp. 123–39

Acker, S. (1994) *Gendered Education*, Buckingham: Open University Press

Adams, C. and Laurikietis, R. (1980) *The Gender Trap: A Closer Look at Sex Roles*, London: Virago in association with Quartet Books

Adams, K. (1990) 'Divide and rule: the marriage ban 1918–1945', in Paterson, F. and Fewell, J. (eds) (1990) *Girls in their Prime: Scottish Education Revisited*, Edinburgh: Scottish Academic Press, pp. 89–108

Beck, U. (1992) *The Risk Society*, London: Sage

Beck, U. (1998) *Democracy Without Enemies*, Cambridge: Polity Press

Bly, R. (1991) *Iron John: A Book About Men*, Shaftesbury: Element

Butler, J. (1990) *Gender Trouble: Feminism and the Subversion of Identity*, New York: Routledge

Carrington, B. and Skelton, C. (2003) 'Re-thinking "role models": equal opportunities in teacher recruitment in England and Wales', *Journal of Education Policy*, Vol. 18, No. 3, pp. 253–65

Coleman, M. (2002) *Women as Head-Teachers: Striking the Balance*, Stoke on Trent: Trentham Books

Connell, R. W. (1989) 'Cool guys, swots and wimps: the interplay of masculinity and education', *Oxford Review of Education*, Vol. 15, No. 30, pp. 291–303

Connell, R. W. (1996) *Masculinities*, Cambridge: Polity Press

Crompton, R. (1997) *Women and Work in Modern Britain*, Oxford: Oxford University Press

Crompton, R. (2006) *Employment and the Family: The Reconfiguration of Work and Family Life in Contemporary Society*, Cambridge: Cambridge University Press

Croxford, L. (2000) 'Gender and national curricula', in Salisbury and Riddell (eds) (2000), pp. 115–33

Davies, B. (2003) 'Death of critique and dissent? The policies and practices of new managerialism and of "evidence-based practice" ', *Gender and Education*, Vol. 15, pp. 89–101

Deem, R. (1998) ' "New managerialism" and higher education: the management of performances and cultures in universities in the United Kingdom', *International Studies in Sociology of Education*, Vol. 8, No. 1, pp. 27–47

Dench, S., Aston, J., Evans, C., Meager, N., Williams, M. and Willison, R. (2002) *Key Indicators of Women's Position in Britain*, London: Women and Equality Unit / DTI

Department of Trade and Industry (2005) *Fairness for All*, London: DTI

Drudy, S., Martin, M., Woods, M. and O'Flynn, J. (2005) *Men in the Classroom: Gender Imbalance in Teaching*, London: Routledge

Etzioni, A. (1969) *The Semi-Professions and their Organisation*, New York: Free Press

European Union (2004) *Key Data on Education in Europe, 2002*, Brussels: European Commission

Evans, K. (2004) 'Genderequal: necessities – possibilities – limits', in *Gender and Qualification EUR 21103*, Luxemburg: European Commission, pp. 89–91

Exworthy, M. and Halford, S. (1999) *Professionals and the New Managerialism in the*

Public Sector, London: Open University Press

Fewell, J. (1990) 'The protection racket: the occupation of the teaching profession', in Paterson, F. and Fewell, J. (eds) (1990) *Girls in their Prime: Scottish Education Revisited*, Edinburgh: Scottish Academic Press, pp. 109–30

Francis, B. (1999) 'Lads, lasses and (New) Labour: 14–16-year-old students' responses to the "laddish behaviour and boys' underachievement" debate', *British Journal of Sociology of Education*, Vol. 20, No. 3, pp. 355–71

Francis, B. (2002) 'Is the future really female? The impact and implications of gender for 14–16 year olds career choices', *Journal of Education and Work*, Vol. 15, pp. 97–110

Francis, B., Hutchings, M. and Archer, L. (2003) 'Subject choice and occupational aspirations among pupils at girls' schools', *Pedagogy, Culture and Society*, Vol. 11, No. 3, pp. 423–40

Franks, S. (1999) *Having None of It: Women, Men and the Future of Work*, London: Granta Books

Gaskell, J. (1992) *Gender Matters from School to Work*, London: Routledge

Gibb, K., Kearns, A., Keoghan, M., Mackay D. and Turok, I. (1998) *Revising the Scottish Area Deprivation Index: Report to the Scottish Office, Final Report*, Vol. 1, Glasgow: Department of Urban Studies, University of Glasgow

Gordon, T. (2006) 'The Nordic approach to the promotion of equality', *Scottish Affairs*, 56, pp. 57–68

Gray, C. and Leith, H. (2004) 'Perpetuating gender stereotypes in the classroom: a teacher perspective', *Educational Studies*, Vol. 30, No. 1, pp. 3–17

Hakim, C. (1995) 'Five feminist myths about women's employment', *British Journal of Sociology*, Vol. 46, No. 3, pp. 429–55

Hakim, C. (1996) *Key Issues in Women's Work*, London: Athlone Press

Hakim, C. (2002) 'Lifestyle preferences as determinants of women's differential labour market careers', *Work and Occupations*, Vol. 29, pp. 428–59

Hakim, C. (2004) *Key Issues in Women's Work: Female Diversity and the Polarisation of Women's Employment* London: Glasshouse Press

Hartmann, H. (1982) 'Capitalism, patriarchy and job segregation by sex', in Giddens, A. and Held, D. (eds) (1982) *Classes, Power and Conflict*, London and Basingstoke: Macmillan, pp. 446–69

Hay, V. and Bradford, S. (2004) 'The return of the repressed? The gender politics of emergent forms of professionalism in education', *Journal of Education Policy*, Vol. 19, No. 6, pp. 691–713

Johnston, J., Mckeown E. and Mcewen, A. (1999) 'Choosing primary teaching as a career: the perspectives of males and females in training', *Journal of Education for Teaching*, Vol. 25, No. 1, pp. 55–64

Kay, H. (2001) *Women and Men in the Professions in Scotland*, Edinburgh: Scottish Executive Central Research Unit

Kimmel, M. (1994) 'Masculinity as homophobia: fear, shame and silence in the construction of gender identity', in Brod, H. and Kaufman, M. (eds) (1994) *Theorising Masculinities*, London: Sage, pp. 119–42

Lortie, D. C. (1975) *Schoolteachers: A Sociological Study*, Chicago: University of Chicago Press

Mccluskey, G., Stead, J., Weedon, E., Kane, J., Lloyd, G. and Riddell, S. (2006) *Restorative Practices in Scottish Schools: Final Report to the Scottish Executive*, Edinburgh: University of Edinburgh

Mac an Ghaill, M. (1994) *The Making of Men, Masculinities, Sexualities and Schooling* Buckingham: Open University Press

Mac an Ghaill, M. (1996) ' "What about the boys?": schooling, class and crisis masculinity' *Sociological Review*, Vol. 44, No. 3, pp. 381–97

Mahony, P. (2000) 'Teacher education policy and gender', in Salisbury and Riddell (eds) (2000), pp. 229–41

Miller, L., Neathey, F., Pollard, E. and Hill, D. (2004) *Occupational Segregation, Gender Gaps and Skill Gaps*, Manchester: Equal Opportunities Commission

Mills, M. (2001) *Challenging Violence in Schools: An Issue of Masculinities*, Buckingham: Open University Press

Mills, M., Martino, W. and Lingard, B. (2004) 'Attracting, recruiting and retaining male teachers: policy issues in the male teacher debate', *British Journal of Sociology of Education*, Vol. 25, No. 3, pp. 355–69

Newman, J. (2000) 'Beyond the new public management? Modernising public sector services', in Clarke, J. and McLaughlin, E. (eds) (2000) *New Managerialism: New Welfare*, London: Open University Press, pp. 45–61

Oakley, A. (1981) *Subject Women*, Oxford: Martin Robertson

Osgood, J., Francis, B. and Archer, L. (2006) 'Gendered identities and work placement: why don't boys care?' *Journal of Education Policy*, Vol. 21, No. 3, pp. 305–21

Ozga, J. and Walker, L. (1999) 'In the company of men', in Whitehead, S. and Moodley, R. (eds) (1999) *Transforming Managers: Gendering Change in the Public Sector*, London: UCL Press, pp. 107–19

Phillips, A. (2004) 'Defending equality of outcome', *Journal of Political Philosophy*, Vol. 12, No. 1, pp 1–19

Rees, T., Heaton, P. and Mcbriar, L. (2000) 'Women head teachers in Northern Ireland', in Salisbury and Riddell (eds) (2000), pp. 208–28

Reynolds, E. (2001) 'Learning the hard way: boys, hegemonic masculinity and the negotiation of identities in the primary school', *British Journal of Sociology of Education*, Vol. 22, No. 3, pp. 369–85

Riddell, S. (1992) *Gender and the Politics of the Curriculum*, London: Routledge

Riddell, S., Tett, L., Burns, C., Ducklin, A., Ferrie, J., Stafford A. and Winterton, M. (2005) *Gender Balance of the Teaching Workforce in Publicly Funded Schools in Scotland*, Edinburgh: Scottish Executive

Riddell, S., Weedon, E., Fuller, M., Healey, M., Hurst, A., Kelly, K. and Piggott, L. (2007, forthcoming) 'Managerialism and equalities: tensions within widening access policy and practice for disabled students in UK universities', *Higher Education*

Roulston, K. and Mills, M. (2000) 'Male teachers in feminised teaching areas: marching to the beat of the men's movement drum?', *Oxford Review of Education*, Vol. 26, No. 2, pp. 221–37

Sachs, J. and Blackmore, J. (1998) ' "You never show you can't cope". Women in school leadership positions managing their emotions', *Gender and Education*, Vol. 10, pp. 265–79

Salisbury, J. and Riddell, S. (eds) (2000) *Gender, Policy and Educational Change: Shifting Agendas in the UK and Europe*, London: Routledge

Scottish Executive (2001) *Better Behaviour, Better Learning*, The Report of the Discipline Task Group, Edinburgh: Scottish Executive Education Department

Scottish Executive (2004) *Statistical Publication: Education Series: Teachers in Scotland 2003*, Edinburgh: Scottish Executive

Scottish Executive (2005a) *Statistics Publication Notice: Education Series: Results of Teacher Workforce Planning for 2005/2006*, Edinburgh: Scottish Executive

Scottish Executive (2005b) *Review of Initial Teacher Education Stage 2: Report of the Review Group*, Edinburgh: Scottish Executive.

Scottish Qualifications Authority (2006) *Standard Grade Entries: Subject by Gender*, Glasgow: SQA

Siltanen, J. (1986) 'Domestic responsibilities and the structuring of employment', in Crompton, R. and Mann, M. (eds) (1986) *Gender and Stratification*, Cambridge: Polity Press, pp. 97–118

Simpson, R. (2004) 'Masculinity at work: the experience of men in female dominated occupations', *Work, Employment and Society*, Vol. 18, No. 2, pp. 349–68

Simpson, R. L. and Simpson, I. H. (1969) 'Women and bureaucracy in the semi-professions', in Etzioni, A. (ed.) (1969) *The Semi-Professions and their Organization*, New York: Free Press, pp. 199–200

Singh, R. (1998) *Gender Autonomy in Western Europe: An Imprecise Revolution*, Basingstoke: Macmillan Press

Skeggs, B. (1997) *Formations of Class and Gender*, London: Sage

Skelton, C. (2002) 'The "feminisation of schooling" or the "remasculinising" of primary education', *International Studies in Sociology of Education*, Vol. 12, pp. 77–96

Skelton, C. (2003) 'Male primary school teachers and perceptions of masculinity', *Educational Review*, Vol. 55, No. 2, pp. 195–209

Thornton, M. and Bricheno, P. (2003) 'Students' reasons for wanting to teach in primary school', *Research in Education*, Vol. 67, pp. 33–43

Tinklin, T., Croxford, L., Ducklin, A. and Frame, B. (2001) *Gender and Pupil Performance in Scotland's Schools*, Edinburgh: Centre for Educational Sociology, University of Edinburgh

Tinklin, T., Croxford, L., Ducklin, A. and Frame, B. (2005) 'Gender and attitudes to work and family roles: the views of young people from the millennium', *Gender and Education*, Vol. 17, No. 2, pp. 129–42

Tisdall, E. K. M. and Riddell, S. (2006) 'School inclusion in Scotland: competing strategies and discourses', *European Journal of Special Needs Education*, 21(4), pp. 363–379

UNESCO (2003) *United Nations Educational Scientific and Cultural Organisation World Education Indicators* (online). Available from URL: www.uis.unesco.org/ev.php?ID=5264_201&ID2+DO_TOPIC (accessed 18 May 2006)

Walby, S. (1986) *Patriarchy at Work*, Cambridge: Polity Press

Weiner, G., Arnot, M. and David, M. (2001) 'Is the future female? Female success, male disadvantage, and changing gender patterns in education', in Halsey, A.H., Lauder, H., Brown, P. and Wells, P. (eds) (2001) *Education: Culture, Economy, Society*, Milton Keynes: Open University Press, pp. 620–31.

Whitehead, S. M. (2002) *Men and Masculinities*, Cambridge: Polity Press

Willis, P. (1976) *Learning to Labour: How Working Class Kids Get Working Class Jobs*, London: Saxon House Books

Index